Contents

Cellular and molecular Biology

Genetics

Evolution

Taxonomy

Human Body

Animal behavior

Plants

Ecology

Cell division
Questions 1-3 :

(A) Anaphase II
(B) Metaphase I
(C) Prophase II
(D) Metaphase II
(E) Prophase I

1. Stage of meiosis during which recombination of genetic material occur
2. Stage of meiosis during which pairs of homologous chromosomes align at the center of the cell
3. Stage of meiosis during which sister chromatids are separated

4. Which of the following does NOT contain membrane of its structure?
(A) Chromosome
(B) Mitochondrion
(C) Golgi body
(D) Chloroplast
(E) Endoplasmic reticulum

5. Meiosis in diploid organisms results in which of the following?
(A) The production of haploid cells
(B) The generation of new alleles
(C) The formation of a zygote
(D) The transmission of adaptive phenotypes
(E) The creation of triploid gametes

6. Which of the following best describes what is meant by the term '' diploid ''
(A) Containing double-stranded DNA
(B) Containing only one copy of each chromosome
(C) Containing pairs of structurally similar choromosomes
(D) Containing pairs of chromosomes with identical DNA sequences
(E) Containing haphazardly arranged genes

7. A scientist studying onion cells notes that after 12 hrs, the amount of DNA in a cell has doubled. Which of the following is the best explanation for this observation ?
(A) Nucleotides have diffused inot the cell against concentration gradient
(B) Metaphase has begun, concentrating chromosomes in the center of the cell
(C) Protein synthesis has stopped, resulting in an overproduction of DNA
(D) New plasma membranes have been formed during cytokinesis
(E) The S phase of the cell has occurred

8. The codon GUG in messenger RNA has been transcribed from which of the following sequences in DNA ?
(A) GAG
(B) CAC
(C) TAT
(D) CTC
(E) ATA

9. Humans doNOT obtain energy from eating cellulose because ?
(A) Breaking down cellulose into glucose somply requires too much energy
(B) Cellulose is incorporated into the cell walls and hence none is left to burn
(C) The required enzyme necessary to hydrolyze cellulose is lacking
(D) Only alpha glucose may enter the glycolytic pathway
(E) The combustion of glucose is not exergonic

10. The main structural framework for the plasma membrane is provided by which of the following molecules ?
(A) Water
(B) Nucleotides
(C) Monosaccharides
(D) Amino acids
(E) Phospholipids

11. In both photosynthesis and respiration, protons are pumped across the membrane during
(A) Chemiosmosis
(B) Photolysis
(C) Photorespiration
(D) Carbon fixation
(E) Glycolysis

Questions 12- 15 :
(A) DNA
(B) tRNA
(C) mRNA
(D) rRNA
(E) RNA polymerase

12. Translated to synthesize protein
13. Transports amino acids during protein synthesis
14. Passed on to progeny cells during cell division
15. Includes a structure called '' anti-codon''

16. All of the following are needed for photosynthesis **except** ?
(A) Light
(B) Glucose
(C) Chlorophyll
(D) Water
(E) Carbon dioxide

17. In animals, mitosis is LEAST likely to play a significant role in which of the following ?
(A) Reproduction of cells
(B) Repair of damaged tissue
(C) Growth of embryonic tissues
(D) Regenration of limbs
(E) Reduction of chromosomes number

18. A somatic cell from a certain organism has a diploid number of 24 When the cell reproduces by cell division how many chromosomes will each daughter cell have
(A) 12
(B) 23
(C) 24
(D) 46
(E) 48

19. What is the effect of crossing-over?
(A) Increased genetic variation
(B) Increased number of sex cells
(C) Increased number of body cells
(D) Increased number of chromosomes
(E) Increased rate of cell division

20. In garden peas, a single gene controls stem length. The recessive allele (t) produces short stems when homozygous. The dominant allele *(T)* produces long stems. A short-stemmed plant is crossed with a heterozygous long-stemmed plant. Which of the following represents the expected phenotypes of the offspring and the ratio in which they will occur?

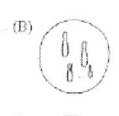

(A) 3 long-stemmed plants : 1 short-stemmed plant
(B) 1 long-stemmed plant : 1 short-stemmed plant
(C) 1 long-stemmed plant : 3 short-stemmed plant
(D) Long-stemmed plants only
(E) Short-stemmed plants only

21. Which of the following represents a typical gamete produced by an organism with a diploid number of 8?

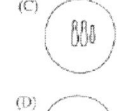

(A) 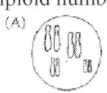
(B)
(C)
(D)
(E)

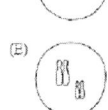

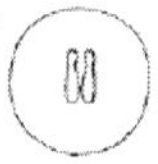

22. Which of the following disease is most likely caused by a mutation in a protein involved in cell cycle regulation?
(A) Diabetes.
(B) Heart disease (clogging of cardiac arteries)
(C) Malaria.
(D) Cancer.
(E) Sickle-cell anemia.

23. Which of the following statements most accurately describes a basic difference between mitosis and meiosis?
(A) Homologous chromosomes form tetrads in mitosis but not in meiosis.
(B) Homologous chromosomes form tetrads in meiosis but not in mitosis.
(C) The nuclear membrane disappears in mitosis but not in meiosis.
(D) A spindle forms in mitosis but not in meiosis.
(E) A spindle forms in meiosis but not in mitosis.

24. Why are male animals able to provide gametes with more genetic diversity than females for reproduction?
(A) Males provide more genes in sperm than females provide in eggs.
(B) Male gametes are produced via meiosis, but female gametes are produced via mitosis.
(C) Crossing over occurs more often in the formation of sperm than in eggs.
(D) Spermatogenesis in males results in four functional sperm, while oogenesis in females results in only one egg and three structures that contain genetic information that is lost when they disintegrate
(E) Sperm that contain a recombination of genes are usually more successful in fertilizing an egg

25. What occurs during meiosis but not mitosis?
(A) Spindles are formed from microtubules.
(B) Chromosome number is conserved.
(C) Homologous chromosomes pair up.
(D) Centromeres split
(E) Cytokinesis

Questions 26-28:

Refer to the following phases of the cell cycle
(A) Anaphase
(B) Interphase
(C) Metaphase
(D) Prophase
(E) Telophase

26. Centromeres align at the equatorial plate
27. Genetic material is replicated
28. Chromosomes are pulled toward opposite poles of the spindle apparatus

29. Which of the following best describes what is meant by the term "diploid"?
(A) Containing double-stranded DNA.
(B) Containing only one copy of each chromosome.
(C) Containing pairs of structurally similar chromosomes.
(D) Containing pairs of chromosomes with identical DNA sequences.
(E) Containing haphazardly arranged genes.

30. If a somatic cell in a diploid organism contains ten pairs of chromosomes, what is the total number of chromatids that are present in the cell after the DNA has replicated but before mitosis has taken place?
(A) 10
(B) 20
(C) 30
(D) 40
(E) 80

Answer:
1. E
2. B
3. A
4. A
5. A
6. C
7. E
8. B
9. C
10. E
11. A
12. C
13. B
14. A
15. B
16. B
17. E
18. C
19. A
20. B
21. B
22. D
23. B
24. D
25. C
26. C
27. B
28. A
29. C
30. D

Cellular and Molecular Biology

Questions 1-4 refer to the following groups of biological compounds.

(A) Proteins
(B) Carbohydrates
(C) Nucleic acids
(D) Lipids
(E) Steroids

1. Synthesized at the ribosome
2. Includes glycogen, chitin, cellulose, and starch
3. Used for insulation and buoyancy in marine Arctic animals
4. Used to carry the genetic code

5. Which of the following pairs of functional groups characterizes the structure of an amino acid?

(A) $-N{<}^H_H$ and $-\overset{O}{\overset{\|}{C}}-R$

(B) $-C{<}^O_{OH}$ and $-N{<}^H_H$

(C) $-C{<}^O_{OH}$ and $-\overset{O}{\overset{\|}{C}}-R$

(D) $-OH$ and $-N{<}^H_H$

(E) $-\overset{O}{\underset{O}{\overset{|}{\underset{|}{C}}}}-H$ and $-N{<}^H_H$

6. The synthesis of protein or carbohydrate polymers always produces which of the following as a by-product?
(A) ATP
(B) O_2
(C) CO_2
(D) Urea
(E) H_2O

Questions 7-10 refer to the diagrams of organic molecules below

(A) [heme structure with Fe]

(B) [glucose structure]

(C) [ATP structure with adenine, ribose, triphosphate]

(D) [cholesterol structure]

(E) [amino acid: H₂N—C(H)(H)—COOH]

7. This molecule is used to transport oxygen A
8. Starch is a polymer of this molecule B
9. This sterol is found in cell membranes and is associated with atherosclerosis D
10. This molecule could result from the hydrolysis of a protein E

Questions 11-14 :

(A) DNA
(B) Cholesterol
(C) Triglyceride
(D) Phospholipid
(E) Protein

11. The major component of the fluid bilayer of a plasma membrane D
12. Main molecule in the plasma membrane A
13. Steroid affecting the fluidity of the plasma membrane B
14. ATP synthase (synthetase) in the inner mitochondrial and chloroplast membranes E

15. Which of the following molecules is a polysaccharide ?
(A) Catalase
(B) Testosterone
(C) Glucose
(D) Glycogen
(E) Hemolglobin

16. Which of th following has the greatest amount of energy per gram ?
(A) Starch
(B) Alanine
(C) Cellulose
(D) Vitamin C
(E) Fat

17. The structural formula above represents which of the following?
(A) A monosaccharide
(B) A glucose molecule
(C) A lipid
(D) An amino acid
(E) A fatty acid

18. Which of the following correctly pairs two of the nucleotide bases that form double-stranded DNA ?
(A) Adenine .... Cytosine
(B) Cytosine.... Guanine
(C) Guanine .... Thymine
(D) Thymine .... Uracil
(E) Uracil ..... Cytosine

19. Proteins are degraded into mixture of amino acids by ?
(A) Osmosis
(B) Diffusion
(C) Hydrolysis
(D) Oxidation
(E) Condensation

20. The conversion of sucrose to glucose and fructose involves the addition of which of the following molecules to the sucrose molecule?
(A) O_2
(B) H_2
(C) ATP
(D) H_2O
(E) NADH

Questions 21-23 refer to the following molecules:
(A) proteins
(B) monosaccharides
(C) lipids
(D) Starch
(E) RNA

21. Contain carbon, hydrogen, and oxygen in a 1:2:1 ratio
22. Are often not soluble in water
23. This group includes enzymes

24. Which of the following molecular characteristics CANNOT be determined from the molecular formula $C_6H_{12}O_6$?
(A) The kind of atoms
(B) The number of atoms
(C) The molecular weight
(D) The position of atoms
(E) The numerical proportion of atoms

25. Which of the following are characteristics of every organic molecule?
I. Very simple structure
II. Contains carbon
III. Contains nitrogen
(A) I only
(B) II only
(C) I and III only
(D) II and III only .
(E) I, II, and III

26. Which of the following is a common characteristic of all lipids?
(A) They are acidic.
(B) They are negatively charged.
(C) They are hydrophobic.
(D) They are made from amino acids.

(E) They are phosphorylated.

27. Which of the following is an amino acid?
(A) $C_3H_6O_3$
(B) $C_6H_{12}O_6$
(C) C_6H_8N
(D) C_2H_5OH
(E) $C_2H_5O_2N$

28. Where on Earth is most organic carbon located?
(A) The atmosphere
(B) Soils
(C) Living organisms
(D) Oceans
(E) Sedimentary rock of marine origin

29. The synthesis of protein or carbohydrate polymers always produces which of the following as a byproduct?
(A) ATP
(B) Oxygen
(C) Carbon dioxide
(D) Urea
(E) Water

30. Which statement about the structure of DNA and RNA is CORRECT?
(A) DNA nucleotides contain phosphate groups and RNA nucleotides do not.
(B) DNA is a non-polar molecule and RNA is a polar molecule.
(C) DNA uses cytosine nucleotides and RNA does not.
(D) DNA contains nitrogen atoms and RNA does not.
(E) DNA contains a different sugar group than RNA

31. A chemical compound formed by combining one adenine molecule, one ribose molecule, and one phosphate group is -
(A) an amino acid
(B) a nucleotide
(C) ATP
(D) RNA
(E) DNA

32. Which of the following is a function of lipids?
(A) Active transport of ions
(B) Long-term energy storage
(C) Oxygen transport
(D) Transcription
(E) DNA replication

33. When maltose is formed from glucose, which of the following occurs?
(A) Water is removed by condensation reaction between glucose molecules
(B) Ionic bonds are formed
(C) A peptide bond is formed
(D) Hydrogen is added to double bonds
(E) A 6-carbon ring structure is converted to a 5-carbon ring structure

Questions 34-37 :

(A) Nucleotide
(B) Amino acid
(C) Lipid
(D) Glucose
(E) Protein

34. A monomer that serves as the building block of polypeptides
35. A building block of DNA
36. A polymer
37. Primary cellular energy source for plants and animals

38. If a Hydrogen atom has 1 proton, 2 neutrons, and 1 electron, then that hydrogen atom is a (an)
(A) Cation
(B) Anion
(C) Isotope
(D) Metal
(E) Electrically charged element

Questions 39-42:

(A) CH₂OH — glucose ring structure

(B) H-N-C-C=O with H, CH₃, OH — amino acid (alanine)

(C) H-C-C-C-C-C=O with H's and OH — fatty acid

(D) H-C-OH, H-C-OH, H-C-OH — glycerol

(E) Phosphate group — Pentose — Nitrogen-containing base (nucleotide)

39. This is a Monosaccharide

40. This compound is necessary for growth and repair

41. Linked to atherosclerosis

42. The Building block of DNA

43. The energy required to run the Calvin cycle reactions of photosynthesis comes from which two substances produced during the light dependent reactions?
(A) ATP and NADPH
(B) ADP and PO4
(C) H⁺ and O₂
(D) O₂ and CO₂
(E) H₂O and CO₂

44. All of the following are correct about enzymes EXCEPT
(A) Enzymes are organic catalysts
(B) Enzymes lower the energy of activation
(C) Enzymes are assisted by cofactors
(D) Enzymes are affected by changes in temperature but not changes in pH
(E) Enzymes are larger than the substrates they work on

45. Which of the following pairs are storage polysaccharides?
(A) Starch and Chitin
(B) Glycogen and Chitin
(C) Glycogen and Starch
(D) Glucagon and Starch
(E) Cellulose and Starch

46. Enzymes function because of their particular shape or conformation. Which level of protein structure is most directly responsible for the shape of a protein?
(A) Primary
(B) Secondary
(C) Tertiary
(D) Quaternary
(E) Cannot be determined

47. Which two cellular organelles in eukaryotes have both electron transport systems and chemiosmotic mechanisms?

(A) Ribosomes and endoplasmic reticulum
(B) Chloroplasts and endoplasmic reticulum
(C) Chloroplasts and mitochondria
(D) Mitochondria and nuclei
(E) Nuclei and Golgi apparatus

48. Which metabolic process is common to both aerobic cellular respiration and alcoholic fermentation?
(A) Krebs cycle
(B) Glycolysis
(C) Electron transport chain
(D) Conversion of pyruvic acid to acetyl CoA
(E) Production of a proton gradient

49. The function of which of the following organelles directly requires oxygen?
(A) Ribosome
(B) Mitochondria
(C) Nucleus
(D) Centriole
(E) Golgi apparatus

Questions 50-54:

(A) Glycolysis
(B) Krebs cycle
(C) Calvin cycle
(D) Light-dependent reactions
(E) Chemiosmosis

50. Process in which O_2 is released as a by-product of redox reactions

51. Process in which CO2 is released as a byproduct of oxidation-reduction reactions

52. Process in which carbon from CO_2 is incorporated into organic molecules

53. Process found in both photosynthesis and cellular respiration

54. Process in which sugar is oxidized to pyruvic acid

55. In a mesophyll cell of a leaf, the synthesis of ATP occurs in which of the following?
 I. Ribosomes
 II. Mitochondria
 III. Chloroplasts
(A) I only
(B) II only
(C) III only
(D) II and III only
(E) I, II, and III

56. Cyanobacteria lack which of the following?
(A) Ribosomes.
(B) Chlorophyll.
(C) A cell membrane.
(D) Mitochondria.
(E) DNA

57. Which of the following does NOT contain a membrane as part of its structure?
(A) Chromosome.
(B) Mitochondrion.
(C) Golgi body.
(D) Chloroplast.
(E) Endoplasmic reticulum

58. Which of the following is a true statement about photosynthesis?
(A) It is initiated by absorption of energy.
(B) It requires nitrogen gas.
(C) It is most efficient in green light.
(D) It occurs only in angiosperms.
(E) It consumes more ATP than it produces

59. The aerobic cellular respiration of glucose is different from the simple burning of glucose in that the aerobic respiration of glucose.
(A) Releases no heat.

(B) Requires no oxygen.
(C) Releases more energy.
(D) Releases hydrocarbons.
(E) Occurs at a lower temperature

60. A gram of which of the following releases the most energy when oxidized?
(A) Amino acid.
(B) Protein
(C) Nucleic acid
(D) Fat
(E) Carbohydrate.

61. Prokaryotes and eukaryotes are both characterized by all of the following EXCEPT:
(A) Ribosomes
(B) Cytoplasm
(C) Mitochondria.
(D) Protein synthesis.
(E) Cell division.

62. An unknown liquid is isolated from a sample of ground-up bean seeds. When the liquid is added to a test tube of water and shaken vigorously, the water and the unknown liquid separate into two layers after a few minutes. To which class of biological molecules should the unknown liquid most likely be assigned ?
(A) Crabohydrates
(B) Enzymes
(C) Lipids
(D) Nucleic acids
(E) Protein

63. The activation energy (E_A) of the reaction is the energy required
(A) To form substrates in the reaction
(B) In change tertiary enzyme structure
(C) To change the bonds in the reactants
(D) To bring reactants together in solution
(E) To allow products to reach a stable state

64. This question is based on the following equation.
$C_6H_{12}O_6 + 6O_2 \rightarrow 6H_2O + 6CO_2 + 38$ ATP

The process shown by the above equation is
(A) reduction and is endergonic
(B) reduction and is exergonic
(C) oxidation and is endergonic
(D) oxidation and is exergonic.
(E) neither oxidation or nor reduction

65. In red blood cells, the enzyme carbonic anhydrase catalyses the following reaction $CO_2 + H_2O \rightarrow H_2CO_3$
Substrates for this reaction include which of the following?
(A) Hemoglobin
(B) H_2CO_3 only
(C) CO_2 only
(D) H_2O only
(E) CO_2 and H_2O

66. Which of the following cells functions without a nucleus?
(A) Nerve cell.
(B) Smooth muscle cell.
(C) Epithelial cell.
(D) Bone cell.
(E) Red blood cell.

67. The major role of enzymes in cells is to.
(A) Alter the rate of chemical reactions.
(B) Alter the normal by-products of chemical reactions.
(C) Control the rate of mutation.
(D) Alter the conductivity of cells.
(E) Serve as the subunits from which proteins are made.

68. All of the following are required for photosynthesis EXCEPT
(A) Chlorophyll.
(B) Light.
(C) Glucose.
(D) Carbon dioxide.
(E) Water.

69. Which of the following properties of water is primarily responsible for its transport in the trunk of a large tree?
(A) Cohesion
(B) Neutral pH
(C) High specific heat
(D) Low molecular weight
(E) Low density as a solid

70. Which step of aerobic respiration produces the most of CO_2?
(A) Glycolysis
(B) The Calvin cycle
(C) The Krebs cycle

(D) Electron transport
(E) ATP synthesis

71. Humans doNOT obtain energy from eating cellulose because ?
(A) Breaking down cellulose into glucose somply requires too much energy
(B) Cellulose is incorporated into the cell walls and hence none is left to burn
(C) The required enzyme necessary to hydrolyze cellulose is lacking
(D) Only alpha glucose may enter the glycolytic pathway
(E) The combustion of glucose is not exergonic

72. In both photosynthesis and respiration, protons are pumped across the membrane during
(A) Chemiosmosis
(B) Photolysis
(C) Photorespiration
(D) Carbon fixation
(E) Glycolysis

73. Which of the following organelles would be present in a eukaryote but NOT in a prokaryote?
I. Nucleus
II. Mitochondria
III. Ribosome

(A) I only
(B) II only
(C) I and II only
(D) II and III only
(E) I, II, III

74.

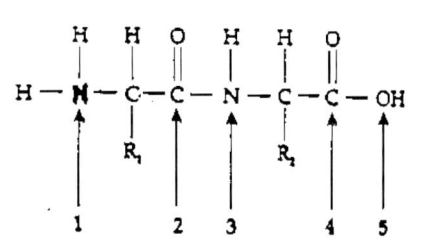

What type of molecule is depicted in the diagram above ?

(A) Protein
(B) Carbohydrate
(C) Lipid
(D) Nucleic acid
(E) Starch

75. If we were to continue adding to this molecule to increase in size, to which atom would the next portion be bonded?
(A) 1
(B) 2
(C) 3
(D) 4
(E) 5

76. The synthesis of this molecule also results in the production of
(A) CO_2
(B) H_2O
(C) Lipid
(D) ATP
(E) $C_6H_{12}O_6$

77. Which metabolic pathway occurs in both fermentation and cellular respiration?
(A) Calvin cycle
(B) Citric acid cycle
(C) Glycolysis
(D) Electron transport chain
(E) Synthesis of water

78. Which chemical bonds are involved in base pairing in DNA?
(A) Covalent bonds
(B) Ionic bonds
(C) Hydrogen bonds
(D) Van der Waals attractions
(E) Polar bonds

79. A student observed an animal cell under a light microscope using a 100X objective. Which of the following organelles could **NOT** be observed by the student?
(A) Lysosomes
(B) Peroxisomes
(C) Mitochondria
(D) Ribosomes
(E) Centrosomes

80. Catalase is an enzyme that accelerates the breakdown of hydrogen peroxide to form water and oxygen gas. If a test tube with catalase and 1% hydrogen peroxide is allowed to stand until no more oxygen is given off, which of the following should be added to make the reaction begin again?
(A) Catalase.
(B) HCl
(C) Hydrogen peroxide.
(D) H_2O
(E) Oxygen

81. Which of the following is a true statement about simple sugars and complex carbohydrates?
I. Both are composed of the same chemical elements.
II. Both are present in equal proportions in most foods.
III. Simple sugars can be assembled into complex carbohydrates.
(A) I only
(B) II only
(C) III only
(D) I and II only
(E) I and III only

82. Vitamins are essential for normal cell function. They are important because they
(A) function as an energy source
(B) are hormones
(C) directly assist in the normal conduction of impulses
(D) resist pH changes
(E) enable enzymes to function normally

83. Which of the following is the best description of a protein molecule ?
(A) Small building blocks called amino acids linked together in one or more chains
(B) Small building blocks called amino acids linked together in a ring
(C) Small building blocks called nucleotides linked together
(D) Small building blocks called monosaccharides linked together in a chain
(E) A glycerol molecule linked to three fatty acids

84. All of the following organic compounds contain a hydroxyl functional group EXCEPT
(A) maltose
(B) glucose
(C) fructose
(D) glycerol
(E) triglyceride

Questions 85-87: refer to the following :

(A) Centrioles
(B) Mitochondria
(C) Nuclei
(D) Plastids
(E) Ribosomes

85. Organelles found in plants but not in animals
86. Organelles found in both eukaryotic and prokaryotic cells
87. Organelles found in animals but not in plants

88. In addition to the single circular chromosome, bacteria may have one or more smaller circular DNA molecules called
(A) Prions
(B) Plasmids
(C) Enzymes
(D) Plasmodium
(E) Provirus

Questions 89-92 :

Three blood samples were prepared according to the following procedure

Sample Y : 1 drop of blood + 10%NaCl	Sample X : 1 drop of blood + 0.85% saline	Sample Z : 1 drop of blood + Distilled water

Slides are made of each sample and the cells are viewed microscopically. The concentration of solutes in the solution used in preparing sample X is the same as that of red blood cells.

89. The blood cells in sample Z would
(A) Look the same as those in solution Y
(B) Undergo lysis
(C) Shrink
(D) Exhibit turgor pressure
(E) Show wilting

90. Which of the following is true regarding the blood cells in sample Y ?

(A) The cells would look like those in sample X when viewed microscopically
(B) The cells would lose water to the surrounding solution
(C) The concentration of the Na^+ and Cl^- Ions in the cell would decrease
(D) The amount of Na^+ entering the cells will equal the amount of Cl^- leaving the cells
(E) The cells would swell

91. The cells in sample X are unaffected because

(A) Sample X is unstable at temperature below 37 °C
(B) Sample X has a higher solute concentration than human plasma
(C) Sample X has the same solute concentration as human plasma
(D) Sample X has the same concentration as seawater from which animals evolved
(E) Red blood cells are selectively impermeable to water

92. The results of experiment illustrate which of the following processes?
(A) Dehydration
(B) Active transport
(C) Cellular homogeneity
(D) Osmosis
(E) Hydrolysis

93. The oxygen produced during photosynthesis comes from which of the following ?
(A) The air plant takes in
(B) Carbon dioxide
(C) Water
(D) Carbohydrates
(E) NO_2^-

94. The nitrogenous base guanine makes up 30% of the bases of DNA of a certain organism. What percentage of this organism's bases is composed of adenine?
(A) 20%
(B) 30%
(C) 40%
(D) 50%
(E) 60%

95. Which of the following does NOT occur in mitochondria ?
(A) Glycolysis
(B) Krebs cycle
(C) ETC
(D) Oxidative phosphorylation
(E) Formation of a proton gradient

96. Chloroplasts are the organelles in which.
(A) There is a net gain of water
(B) Cell division is controlled
(C) Large molecules are packed for export
(D) Light energy is converted to chemical energy
(E) Degredation of organelles occurs

97. Bacterial, fungal, algal, and plants cells have fixed shapes because they have
(A) A plasma membrane
(B) A cell wall
(C) A large central vacuole
(D) Mitochondria
(E) Chloroplasts

98. Which of the following substances are produced by the light reactions of photosynthesis?
(A) ATP and NADPH
(B) ATP and glucose
(C) NaOH and glucose
(D) ATP and NADH
(E) NADPH and glucose

99. All of the following is true about RNA EXCEPT
(A) It is single stranded
(B) Its bases are adenine, thymine, guanine, and uracil
(C) It has a sugar-phosphate backbone
(D) Its sugar is ribose
(E) It is found in both in nucleus and the cytoplasm of the cell

100. The function of golgi apparatus is to
(A) Package and store proteins for secretion
(B) Synthesize proteins
(C) Function in cellular respiration
(D) Help the cell expel waste
(E) Digest foreign substances

101. The location on an enzyme where substrate binds is called the
(A) Binding site
(B) Reaction center
(C) Allosteric site
(D) Lock-and-key model
(E) Active site

102. Two beakers of water are placed on a windowsill where they are exposed to sunlight. One beaker contains several sprigs of an aquatic plant, and the second beaker contains only water. The oxygen levels of the water in both beakers are periodically measured. In the beaker containing the plant, the oxygen level increases during the daylight hours and decreases steadily after sunset. The oxygen level in the second beaker remains stable. Which of the following statements best explains the changing oxygen levels in the beaker with the plant?

(A) An increase in carbon dioxide causes a decrease in oxygen.
(B) In the absence of light, oxygen becomes less soluble.
(C) During the day, plants produce more oxygen by photosynthesis than they use in respiration
(D) Plants carry on respiration only at night.
(E) Plants take in carbon dioxide and give off oxygen

103. What structure is common to ALL cell types?
(A) Chloroplast
(B) Plasma membrane
(C) Cell wall
(D) Mitochondria
(E) Flagella

Questions 104-106: refer to the following experiment and results obtained. Dialysis bags are semi-permeable membranes, allowing the transport of small molecules while prohibiting larger ones. In an experiment, students filled dialysis bags with different concentrations of sucrose solution and placed them in a beaker of distilled water. The bags were each weighed before being placed in the beaker. After two minutes, they were removed from the beaker, dried, and weighed again

104. Which dialysis bag experiences the largest percent change in mass?
(A) 0.2 M sucrose
(B) 0.4 M sucrose
(C) 0.6 M sucrose
(D) 0.8 M sucrose
(E) M sucrose

105. If the 0.6 M sucrose solution bag was left in the beaker for four minutes, all of the following occur **EXCEPT**
(A) Mass of dialysis bag increases to more than 30.1 g
(B) Water travels down its concentration gradient
(C) Decrease in the bag's molarity of sucrose
(D) Sucrose leaks into the beaker
(E) Volume of water in the beaker decreases

106. Glucose molecule is small enough to pass through the bag. If glucose was substituted for sucrose in the dialysis experiment above, by what process does it cross the membrane?
(A) Osmosis
(B) Active transport
(C) Simple diffusion
(D) Facilitated diffusion
(E) Transcription

107. The products of the light reactions, or photophosphorylation, in photosynthesis are
(A) oxygen and water
(B) oxygen and ATP
(C) oxygen, ATP, and NADPH
(D) water, ATP, and NADPH
(E) water, ATP, and $NADP^+ + H^-$

108. Which of the following can be used to distinguish prokaryotes from eukaryotes?
(A) Prescence of cell membrane
(B) Prescence of a flagellum
(C) Prescence of ribosomes
(D) Prescenece of cytoskeleton
(E) Prescene of chloroplasts

109. The plasma membrane of eukaryotic cell function in the
(A) Synthesis of lipids and steroid hormones
(B) Polymerization of proteins
(C) Breakdown of hydrogen peroxide and ammonia
(D) Release of energy from carbohydrates and fats
(E) Regulation of nutrients entering and leaving the cell

110. Lactic acid in humans is a product formed as a result of which of the following processes?
(A) Breakdown of nucleic acids
(B) Breakdown of protein in digestion activity of muscle cells when oxygen supply is insufficient
(C) Activity of muscle cells when oxygen supply is insufficient
(D) Release of stomach acids during development of an ulcer
(E) Reaction of fats with phosphorus compounds

111. A protein synthesized in the cytoplasm and transported to the plasma membrane. Which of the following summarizes the protein's pathway in the cell?
(A) Smooth endoplasmic reticulum → nucleus → vesicle → plasma membrane
(B) Plastid → rough endoplasmic reticulum → plasma membrane
(C) Nucleus → vesicle → rough endoplasmic reticulum → plasma membrane
(D) Smooth endoplasmic reticulum → microfilament → vesicle → plasma membrane
(E) Rough endoplasmic reticulum → golgi complex → vesicle → plasma membrane

112. Which cell organelle shows prokaryotic cell structure and has been proposed as providing evidence of endosymbiosis?
(A) Golgi apparatus
(B) mitochondrion
(C) nucleolus
(D) ribosome
(E) Nucleus

113. A solution that has a higher concentration of solute than another solution is called:
(A) hypertonic
(B) hypotonic
(C) isotonic
(D) concentration
(E) Osmotic

114. Which of the following is true about DNA and RNA in eukaryotes?
(A) DNA is found only in the nucleus; RNA is found only in the cytoplasm.
(B) DNA is energy-storage compound; RNA is used for replication of DNA.
(C) DNA is typically single stranded; RNA is typically double stranded.
(D) DNA contains uracil; RNA contains thymine
(E) DNA is transcribed; RNA is translated

Questions 115-118:

(A) DNA
(B) tRNA
(C) mRNA
(D) rRNA
(E) RNA polymerase

115. Translated to synthesize protein
116. Transports amino acids during protein synthesis
117. Passed on to progeny cells during cell division
118. Includes a structure known as the "anticodon."

119. The electron transport chain pumps protons
(A) out of the mitochondrial matrix.
(B) out of the intermembrane space and into the matrix.
(C) out of the mitochondrion and into the cytoplasm.
(D) out of the cytoplasm and into the mitochondrion
(E) Out of the mitochondrion and into the nucleus

120. What process of cellular respiration generates the most ATP?
(A) glycolysis
(B) oxidation of pyruvate
(C) Krebs cycle
(D) Chemiosmosis
(E) Light dependent reaction

121. The bases of RNA are the same as those of DNA with the exception that RNA contains
(A) cysteine instead of cytosine.
(B) uracil instead of thymine.
(C) cytosine instead of guanine.
(D) uracil instead of adenine
(E) Uracil instead of guanine

122. Which of the following statements is **not true** of prokaryotic cells?
(A) Prokaryotic cells are multicellular
(B) Prokaryotic cells do not have a nucleus
(C) Prokaryotic cells have circular DNA
(D) Prokaryotic cells have flagella
(E) Prokaryotic cells do not have mitochondria

123. The prokaryotic genome is contained in the
(A) plasmid
(B) endospore
(C) pilus
(D) nucleoid region
(E) Mitochondria

124. The oxygen produced during photosynthesis comes from which of the following?
(A) The air the plant takes in.
(B) Carbon dioxide.
(C) Water.
(D) Carbohydrates.
(E) Nitrates

125. What structure is common to ALL cell types?
(A) Chloroplast
(B) Plasma membrane
(C) Cell wall
(D) Mitochondria
(E) Flagella

126. The products of the light reactions, or photophosphorylation, in photosynthesis are
(A) oxygen and water
(B) oxygen and ATP
(C) oxygen, ATP, and NADPH
(D) water, ATP, and NADPH.
(E) water, ATP, and $NADP^+ + H^+$

127. A culture of animal cell and a culture of plant cells are pulverized and tested for the presence of several different molecules. Which of the following molecules should be siginificantly more prevalent in the plant cell sample?

(A) Glucose
(B) Deoxyribonucleic acid
(C) Adenosine triphosphate
(D) Cholesterol
(E) Cellulose

128. You are told that an unidentified cell contains a single, circular DNA molecule but no defined nucleus. Which of the following is it also possible for the cell to possess?

I. Chloroplasts
II. Cell wall
III. Ribosomes
(A) I only
(B) III only
(C) I and II only
(D) II and III only
(E) I ,II and III

129. In a eukaryotic cell, where can DNA be found?
(A) Ribosomes and nucleus
(B) Nucleus only
(C) Nucleus and mitochondria
(D) Golgi complex only
(E) Cytoplasm

130. Here is a sketch. All of the following processes produce this molecule EXCEPT the

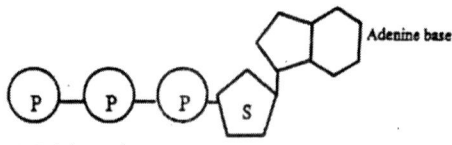

(A) Calvin cycle
(B) Krebs cycle
(C) Electron transport chain
(D) Light-dependent reactions
(E) Glycolysis

131. A bag made of a flexible semi-permeable membrane is filled with a glucose and starch solution. Like cell membranes, this bag is permeable to water and glucose but not to starch. The bag is suspended in a beaker containing a 10% glucose solution. In 30 minutes bag can be expected to

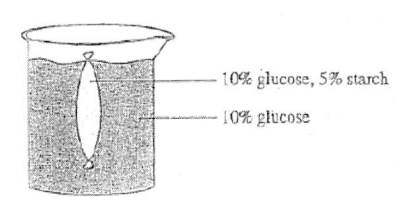

(A) Swell.
(B) Shrink slightly.
(C) Collapse entirely.
(D) Become impermeable to glucose.
(E) Remain the same

132. The primary role of a lysosome is:
(A) intracellular digestion.
(B) ATP synthesis.
(C) lipid transport.
(D) carbohydrate storage.
(E) protein synthesis

133. Which statement about chloroplasts is **FALSE**?
(A) They are organelles with a double membrane.
(B) They contain their own genetic information and ribosomes.
(C) They are found in eukaryotic and prokaryotic cells.
(D) The thylakoid membranes within the chloroplast contain chlorophyll.
(E) They contain ATP

134. _____ bonds are important components that hold DNA strands together in the DNA double helix. (fill in the blank)
(A) Ionic
(B) Covalent
(C) Polar covalent
(D) Peptide
(E) Hydrogen

135. Two beakers of water are placed on a windowsill where they are exposed to sunlight. One beaker contains several sprigs of an aquatic plant, and the second beaker contains only water. The oxygen levels of the water in both beakers are periodically measured. In the beaker containing the plant, the oxygen level increases during the daylight hours and decreases steadily after sunset. The oxygen level in the second beaker remains stable. Which of the following statements best explains the changing oxygen levels in the beaker with the plant?

(A) An increase in carbon dioxide causes a decrease in oxygen.
(B) In the absence of light, oxygen becomes less soluble.
(C) During the day, plants produce more oxygen by photosynthesis than they use in respiration.
(D) Plants carry on respiration only at night.
(E) Plants take in carbon dioxide and give off oxygen.

136. Which of the following contain N and P as component elements in addition to C, H and O?
(A) Haemoglobin and chitin
(B) Phopholipids and DNA
(C) Albumin and inulin
(D) Phopholipids and chitin
(E) RNA and collagen

137. What occurs when fat is synthesized?
(A) One fatty acid and one glycerol molecule are hydrolysed
(B) Three fatty acid molecules combine with a molecule of glycerol to produce a molecule of fat plus three molecules of water.
(C) Three fatty acid molecules are hydrolysed by three molecules of water and one molecule of glycerol to produce a fat molecule.
(D) One fatty acid and one glycerol molecule are condensed.
(E) All bonds between the carbon atoms in the hydrocarbon chain become single bonds

138. Which statement is **CORRECT**?

(A) Animal cells have mitochondria and no chloroplasts; plant cells have chloroplasts and no mitochondria.
(B) Energy is produced in the mitochondrion in the form of ATP and does not involve an electron transport chain; energy produced in the chloroplasts involves a light-activated electron transport chain
(C) Oxygen is released by the Calvin cycle during photosynthesis.
(D) Pyruvate is the end product of the Krebs (citric acid) cycle.
(E) Chloroplasts and mitochondria both produce ATP through the process of chemiosmosis

139. If a typical animal cell with an intracellular fluid containing 0.9 percent solutes is placed in distilled water, the cell will.
(A) Undergo mitosis.
(B) Undergo plasmolysis.
(D) Excrete proteins
(C) Remain unchanged in size
(E) Swell and burst

140. Which of the following is true about the production of starch from monosaccharides?
(A) Carbon dioxide is produced as a by-product
(B) The formation of peptide bonds is required.
(C) Water is produced as a by-product.
(D) The reactions occur only in animal cells.
(E) It can only occur during photosynthesis.

141. Which of the following would be found within an autotrophic eukaryotic cell (and not a heterotrophic eukaryotic cell)?
(A) Mitochondria
(B) Ribosomes
(C) Rough endoplasmic reticulum
(D) Chlorophyll
(E) Vacuole

142. Which statement accurately describes essential amino acids?
(A) They are the only amino acids required for life.
(B) They are the only amino acids to contain sulphur (sulfur).
(C) They can only be obtained by eating meat.
(D) They are the only amino acids required in protein synthesis.
(E) They cannot be manufactured by an organism's body

143. In a eukaryotic cell, where does the synthesis of DNA, RNA, and proteins occur? (ER = endoplasmic reticulum)

	DNA	RNA	Proteins
a.	nucleus	nucleus	nucleus
b.	nucleus	cytosol	cytosol + ER
c.	nucleus	nucleus	cytosol + ER
d.	cytosol	cytosol	nucleus
e.	cytosol	nucleus	cytosol + ER

144. When *Streptococcus pneumonia* is exposed to an antibiotic, bacteria try to pump the antibiotic out of their cell interior. Which mechanism is most likely used by bacteria to pump the antibiotic out?
(A) Diffusion
(B) Facilitated diffusion
(C) Osmosis
(D) Active transport
(E) Symport (when two different molecules move in the same direction)

145. Which of the following best supports the hypothesis that mitochondria are descendants of endosymbiotic bacteria cells?
(A) Mitochondria and bacteria possess similar ribosomes and DNA.
(B) Mitochondria and bacteria possess similar nuclei.
(C) Glycolysis occurs in both mitochondria and bacteria.
(D) Both mitochondria and bacteria have microtubules.
(E) Both mitochondria and photosynthetic bacteria possess chloroplasts

146. All of the following are associated with the Krebs cycle EXCEPT
(A) Carbon dioxide is produced from the chemical rearrangement of citric acid
(B) Energy is released and used to form ATP molecules
(C) Light energy in the green-yellow wavelengths is absorbed and utilized
(D) Specific enzymes for each reaction are found within the mitochondrion
(E) Hydrogen ions and electrons are transferred to the carrier NAD^+

147. Which property of water accounts for its moderating effects on the Earth's atmosphere?
(A) Cohesive
(B) Thermal
(C) Transparency
(D) Adhesive
(E) Hydrogen bonding

148. All of the following are part of the cytoskeleton EXCEPT
(A) microtubules
(B) microfilaments
(C) flagella
(D) cilia
(E) ribosomes

149. Which are functions of lipids?
(A) Hydrophilic solvent and energy storage
(B) Hydrophobic solvent and membrane potential
(C) Thermal insulation and energy storage
(D) Thermal insulation and hydrophilic solvent
(E) Protein synthesis

150. What is light energy used for in photolysis?
(A) Formation of hydrogen and oxygen
(B) Formation of carbon dioxide only
(C) Formation of ATP and glucose
(D) Formation of oxygen only
(E) Formation of water

151. Which statement accurately describes essential amino acids?
(A) They are the only amino acids required for life.
(B) They are the only amino acids to contain sulphur (sulfur)
(C) They can only be obtained by eating meat.
(D) They are the only amino acids required in protein synthesis.
(E) They cannot be manufactured by an organism's body.

152. Which of the following is NOT a true statement about water?
(A) In living organisms, the hydrolysis of polymers to monomers uses water.
(B) Autotrophs split water and produce oxygen gas.
(C) The specific heat of water stabilizes the temperature of ocean water.
(D) During photosynthesis, water is converted into carbon dioxide.
(E) Transport of water in plants occurs because of the cohesive nature of water.

153. Which of the following is a general characteristic of sugars?
(A) They have carbon, hydrogen, and oxygen atoms.
(B) They are hydrophobic because they contain carbon atoms.
(C) They have equal numbers of hydrogen and carbon atoms.
(D) They contain a large amount of phosphate.
(E) They can be bonded together to make proteins.

154. When plant cells are placed in a saltwater solution, the volume of the cytoplasm decreases. Which of the following is the best explanation for this observation?
(A) Cytoplasm leaks out through the cell wall.
(B) The organelles in the cytoplasm are destroyed as the salt enters the cell.
(C) The water, especially in the vacuole, leaves the cell.
(D) Water from outside the cell fills the space between the cell wall and the plasma membrane.
(E) The nucleus explodes and therefore takes up less space in the cytoplasm

155.

Which of the following is correct about the phospholipid shown above?
(A) Only I would be found in the middle of the lipid bilayer.
(B) Only II would be found in the middle of the lipid bilayer.
(C) Both I and II would be found in the middle of the lipid bilayer.
(D) II is hydrophilic.
(E) I and II are hydrophobic.

156. The following statements about the structure of DNA are all true **except** which one?

(A) There are always equal amounts of guanine and cytosine nucleotides
(B) Purine bases pair with pyrimidine bases
(C) Uracil pairs with adenine
(D) Phosphodiester bonds link adjacent nucleotides
(E) Hydrogen bonds are the major forces that maintain a double helix structure

157. If one could suddenly remove all the protein molecules from the plasma membrane of a cell (without destroying the cell), which of the following would one expect to happen?

(A) Transport of all molecules across the plasma membrane would stop
(B) Transport of most ions across the plasma membrane would stop
(C) The amount of cholesterol in the plasma membrane would decrease
(D) Amino acids would rapidly aggregate on the plasma membrane and replace the missing proteins
(E) Large macromolecules would diffuse out of the cell

158. What structures are part of an *Escherichia coli* cell?

(A) Ribosomes, nucleoid and Golgi apparatus
(B) Ribosomes, mitochondria and pili
(C) Cell wall, plasma membrane and nuclear membrane
(D) Pili, flagella and cytoplasm
(E) Cell membrane, chloroplast and E.R

159. Molecules A and B are amino acids and C is a dipeptide. Which reaction represents a condensation reaction?
(A) A + B + H2O → C
(B) A + B → C + H2O
(C) C + H2O → A + B
(D) C → A + B + H2O
(E) A+B+C → H2O

160. ATP is a compound

(A) Low in energy
(B) Without adenine
(C) With ribose
(D) Without phosphate
(E) With deoxyribose

161. Which cell type would probably provide the best opportunity to study lysosomes?
(A) muscle cell.
(B) nerve cell.
(C) phagocytic white blood cell.
(D) leaf cell of a plant.
(E) Pancreatic cell

162. Which one of the following cell structures **doesn't** contain nucleic acid:
(A) mitochondria.
(B) nucleus.
(C) rough endoplasmic reticulum.
(D) smooth endoplasmic reticulum.
(E) chloroplast

163. Which statement is **FALSE**?

(A) If a lysosome bursts, its contents can seriously damage the cytoplasm of a cell.
(B) Chloroplasts and mitochondria are each bounded by two membranes.
(C) Macromolecules may be taken up into a cell by the process of endocytosis.
(D) Protein molecules that are synthesized by rough endoplasmic reticulum are commonly modified in the Golgi apparatus.
(E) In a hypertonic solution, a cell from a multicellular animal usually will swell and burst

164. If you could suddenly remove all the protein molecules from the plasma membrane of a cell (without destroying the cell), which of the following would you expect to happen?

(A) Transport of all molecules across the plasma membrane would stop.
(B) Transport of most ions across the plasma membrane would stop.
(C) The amount of cholesterol in the plasma membrane would decrease.
(D) Amino acids would rapidly aggregate on the plasma membrane and replace the missing proteins.
(E) Large macromolecules would diffuse out of the cell.

Answer:
1. A
2. B
3. D
4. C
5. B
6. E
7. A
8. B
9. D
10. E
11. D
12. D
13. B
14. E
15. D
16. E
17. D
18. B
19. C
20. D
21. B
22. C
23. A
24. D
25. B
26. C
27. E
28. C
29. E
30. E
31. B
32. B
33. A
34. B
35. A
36. E
37. D
38. C
39. A
40. B
41. C
42. E
43. A
44. D
45. C
46. C
47. C
48. B
49. B
50. D
51. B
52. C
53. E
54. A
55. D
56. D
57. A
58. A
59. E
60. D
61. C

62.C	93.C
63.C	94.A
64.D	95.A
65.E	96.D
66.E	97.B
67.A	98.A
68.C	99.B
69.A	100.A
70.C	101.E
71.C	102.C
72.A	103.B
73.C	104.E
74.A	105.D
75.D	106.C
76.B	107.C
77.C	108.D
78.C	109.E
79.D	110.C
80.C	111.E
81.E	112.B
82.E	113.A
83.A	114.E
84.E	115.C
85.D	116.B
86.E	117..A
87.A	118.B
88.B	119.B
89.B	120.D
90.B	121.B
91.C	122.A
92.D	123.D

124.C
125.B
126.C
127.E
128.D
129.C
130.A
131.A
132.A
133.C
134.E
135.C
136.B
137.B
138.E
139.E
140.C
141.D
142.E
143.C
144.D
145.A
146.C
147.B
148.E
149.C
150.A
151.E
152.D
153.A
154.C

155.B
156.C
157.B
158.D
159.B
160.C
161.C
162.D
163.E
164.B

Ecology

1. Which of the following is true concerning the energy in a food web?
(A) Herbivores obtain more energy from food than do carnivores.
(B) Carnivores get the most energy, because they are at the top of the pyramid
(C) The organisms at the top level are larger because they eat organisms from different energy levels
(D) Most of the energy is lost at each step of the food chain
(E) Each animal must make its own energy to survive

Questions 2-3 A population of Paramecium caudatum has the following growth curve on a logarithmic scale.

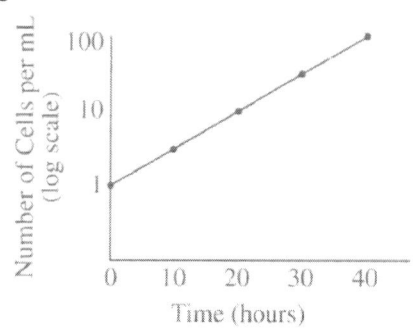

2. The rate of growth of this population is
(A) Exponential. ✓
(B) Additive.
(C) Stepwise.
(D) Logistic.
(E) Hyperbolic.

3. The observed pattern of population increase results from growth in an environment that is.
(A) Deteriorating.
(B) Patchy.
(C) Nonlimiting.
(D) Linear.
(E) Unpredictable.

4. What is the characteristic of the biomass at each successive trophic level of an ecosystem?
(A) It increases, due to the reproduction of plants and animals.
(B) It increases, due to the constant uptake of energy from the sun.
(C) It remains the same, due to the balance of births and deaths.
(D) It decreases, due to the conversion of food energy to heat energy by organisms. ✓
(E) It decreases, due to the shorter life span of top consumers.

5. An isolated population will always decrease in size when
(A) Some individuals are starving
(B) The ratio of death rate to birth rate is greater than one ✓
(C) The carrying capacity of the environment is reached
(D) More males than females are born in the population
(E) Each set of parents has two offspring

6. Which of the following lists includes only abiotic factors of an ecosystem?
(A) Maples, oaks, and phytoplankton
(B) Cattails, pond lilies, and atmospheric gases
(C) Sunlight, water, and amphibians
(D) Producers, consumers, and decomposers
(E) Water, soil, minerals, and sunlight ✓

7. Plants that form flowers that are not brightly colored and that lack fragrance are most likely pollinated by.
(A) Bees.
(B) Wind.
(C) Birds.
(D) Butterflies.
(E) Flies.

8. Which of the following pairs does **NOT** match?

(A) Tropical rainforest – high species diversity
(B) Ozone shield depletion – increased radiation reaching the surface of Earth
(C) Greenhouse effect – rise in atmospheric CO2
(D) Eutrophication – decreased net primary productivity
(E) Acid rain – rain with pH < 5.0

9. In pheasant, males are larger and have more colourful plumage than females. Which of the following is most likely to account for these differences between males and females?
(A) Natural selection
(B) Risk of predation
(C) Mimicry
(D) Sexual selection
(E) Niche differences between the sexes

10. Which of the following organisms serve as decomposers in the ecosystem?
(A) Bacteria and viruses
(B) Fungi and bacteria
(C) Viruses and protists
(D) Fungi and viruses
(E) Bacteria and plants

11. The portion of the earth that is inhabited by life is known as the
(A) ecosystem
(B) biosphere
(C) biome
(D) population
(E) community

Questions 12-15 :

(A) Taiga
(B) Tundra
(C) Grassland
(D) Tropical rain forest
(E) Temperate deciduous forest

12. The biome at the highest latitude
13. The biome characterized by harsh winters, short summers, and evergreen trees
14. The biome with producers that are adapted to fires
15. The biome with the greatest species diversity

16. Which of these ecosystems accounts for the largest amount of earth's nutritional resources?
(A) oceans
(B) tropical rain forest
(C) taiga
(D) grasslands
(E) temperate deciduous forest

17. Which of the following is a detritivore?
(A) Moss
(B) Diatoms
(C) Mushroom
(D) Corn
(E) Fern

18. Plants may use the ammonia (NH3) released by nitrogen fixing bacteria to synthesize all of the following EXCEPT
(A) Cytosine
(B) Methionine
(C) Enzymes
(D) Carrier proteins
(E) Cellulose

19. The relationship between legumes and nitrogen-fixing bacteria demonstrates
(A) Mutualism
(B) Commensalism
(C) Parasitism
(D) Predation
(E) Convergent evolution

20. The process by which some bacteria transform ammonia (NH^3) into gaseous N^2 in the atmosphere is called
(A) Transpiration
(B) Nitrogen fixation
(C) Denitrification
(D) Ammonifying
(E) Nitrification

21. Of the following, what best explains how animals obtain the nitrogen and amino acids they require to survive?
(A) By eating plants that have obtained nitrogen from bacteria or other animals that have eaten these plants
(B) By ingesting nitrogen-fixing bacteria from soil
(C) Through simple respiration of nitrogen in the atmosphere, absorbed either through skin or lungs
(D) By providing nitrogen-fixing bacteria a habitat within their own bodies
(E) By drinking water that contains dissolved nitrogen

Questions 22-24 :
(A) Carnivores
(B) Decomposers
(C) Herbivores
(D) Producers
(E) Omnivores

22. Bacteria that convert the excrement of cattle into simpler substances
23. Rotifers that eat unicellular green algae
24. Minnows that eat only larvae

25. A major role of certain bacteria in ecosystems is the conversion of.
(A) Nitrogen to ammonia.
(B) Oxygen to ozone.
(C) Sodium to sodium chloride.
(D) Hydrogen to water.
(E) Calcium carbonate to carbon dioxide

26. An organism's niche is :
(A) The range of temperatures that the organism needs to survive
(B) A full description of the place an organism lives
(C) The range of physical and biological conditions in which an organism lives and the way it obtains what it needs to survive and reproduce
(D) All the physical factors in the organism's environment
(E) All the biological factors in the organism's environment

27. The lowest level of environmental complexity that includes living and non-living factors is:
(A) Ecosystem
(B) Biosphere
(C) Biome
(D) Community
(E) Population

28. Which of. the following biomes tends to have the greatest temperature swings?
(A) tropical rain forest
(B) temperate deciduous forest
(C) taiga
(D) desert
(E) ocean

29. Which of the following is the best example of an ecological community ?
(A) All of the pigeons inhabiting a city
(B) A school of trout in the Mississippi river
(C) Tropical rain forests worldwide and all of the organisms that inhabit them
(D) All of the plants, nsects, rodents and predators inhabiting a small island
(E) An ant colony

30. The prairie of North America and the steppe of Russia-both grasslands-are examples of the same
(A) Biome
(B) Biopsy
(C) Biosphere
(D) Community
(E) Niche

31. A boy goes to visit his grandparents. As he drives along, he sees man-birch, oak, and maple trees that are losing their leaves. What biome type is the boy visiting?
(A) Tropical rainforest
(B) Desert
(C) Taiga
(D) Temperate deciduous forest
(E) Savanna

32. Which of the following is a density-independent factor?
(A) Disease
(B) Famine
(C) Floods
(D) Predation
(E) Increase in toxins in the environment

Questions 33-35 :

Whale

Duck

Shark

Starfish

Dinosaur

33. Which of the following is the correct sequence of animals that appeared first?
(A) Shark-starfish-dinosour-duck-whale
(B) Starfish-shark-dinosaur-duck-whale
(C) Starfish-dinosaur-shark-duck-whale
(D) Dinosaur-starfish-shark-duck-whale
(E) Duck-starfish-shark-dinosaur-whale

34. Which of the following animals excrete uric acid?
(A) Starfish and dinosaur
(B) Shark and whale
(C) Duck and shark
(D) Dinosaur and shark
(E) Dinosaur and duck

35. Which of following animals represent covergent evolution?
(A) Whale and duck
(B) Shark and duck
(C) Starfish and dinosaur
(D) Shark and whale
(E) Starfish and shark

36. Which of these ecosystems accounts for the largest amount of earth's nutritional resources?
(A) oceans
(B) tropical rain forest
(C) taiga
(D) grasslands
(E) temperate deciduous forest

37. At the end of each geologic time periods, large number of species, genera and even families of animals disappeared from the fossil record. This observation best exemplifies
(A) Convergent evolution.
(B) Gradualistic evolution.
(C) Genetic drift.
(D) Mass extinction.
(E) Adaptive radiation

Questions 38-41 :

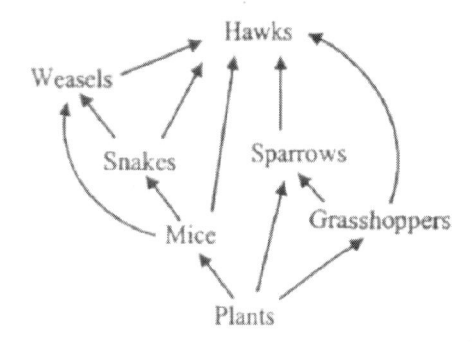

[Food web diagram: Plants → Mice, Grasshoppers; Grasshoppers → Sparrows, Hawks; Mice → Snakes, Weasels, Hawks; Snakes → Hawks, Weasels; Sparrows → Hawks; Weasels → Hawks]

38. Which of the following organisms act as omnivores in the food web?
(A) Hawks.
(B) Sparrows.
(C) Weasels.
(D) Snakes.
(E) Grasshoppers

39. Of the following pairs of organism in the food web, which are involved both in a predator-prey relationship with each other and in competition with each other for food?
(A) Snakes and mice.
(B) Snakes and sparrows
(C) Plants and grasshoppers.
(D) Hawks and grasshoppers.
(E) Hawks and weasels.

40. All of the following organisms may act as secondary consumers in the food web EXCEPT
(A) Sparrows.
(B) Snakes.
(C) Mice.
(D) Weasels.
(E) Hawks

41. What is the maximum number of trophic levels in this food web?
(A) 3
(B) 4
(C) 5
(D) 7
(E) 12

42. In a food chain, the concentration of some environmental pollutants increases with trophic level. For example, in a particular food chain, the DDT concentration in zooplankton is 0.04 ppm, in small fish it is 0.5 ppm, and in fisheating birds it is 25 ppm. This phenomenon is referred to as
(A) Active concentration.
(B) Active transport.
(C) Bioremediation.
(D) Biomagnification.
(E) Primary production

43. The diagram below represents a biomass pyramid

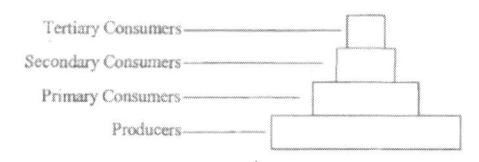

[Biomass pyramid diagram with levels labeled: Tertiary Consumers, Secondary Consumers, Primary Consumers, Producers]

Which of the following is a true statement concerning the energy in this pyramid?
(A) Decomposers are the main source of energy for this pyramid.
(B) Compared to the other trophic levels, the producers contain the least amount of energy
(C) The amount of energy available to tertiary consumers is considerably less than for primary consumers.
(D) Stored chemical bond energy is greater in tertiary consumers than in primary consumers.
(E) Tertiary consumers contain the greatest amount of energy in the system

Questions 44-46
(A) Decomposers (e.g., bacteria)
(B) Producers (e.g., grasses)
(C) Primary consumers (e.g., mice)
(D) Secondary consumers (e.g., snakes)
(E) Tertiary consumers (e.g., hawks)

44. Organisms that comprise the greatest mass of living substance (biomass) in a terrestrial food chain

45. Organisms that convert nitrogen-containing organic molecules into nitrates

46. Organisms that are carnivores and preys at the same time

47. The prediction that the Earth's climate will warm in the next 100 years is based on which of the following observations?
I. Dust and particles are increasing in the upper atmosphere.
II. Carbon dioxide is increasing in the atmosphere.
III. Methane gas is increasing in the atmosphere
(A) I only
(B) II only
(C) III only
(D) I and II only
(E) II and III only

48. According to the diagram, CO_2 in the atmosphere is directly taken up by which of the following?
I. Animals
II. Plants
III. Decomposers
IV. Marine algae

(A) I only
(B) II only
(C) I and III only
(D) II and IV only
(E) I, II and III only

49. Which of the following biomes is most likely to contain maples, gray squirrels, and black bears?
(A) Savanna.
(B) Tundra.
(C) Temperate grassland
(D) Tropical rain forest.
(E) Temperate deciduous forest.

50. Some insect species resemble other insect species that are poisonous or distasteful. This is an example of
(A) Mutation.
(B) Transformation.
(C) Inbreeding.
(D) Mimicry.
(E) Homology.

51. Tundra is different from taiga in that the
(A) Tundra subsoil remains permanently frozen.
(B) Tundra has more rainfall.
(C) Tundra has more trees.
(D) Taiga has a lower mean annual temperature.
(E) Taiga has long, wet summers.

52. Which of the following pairs of organisms are LEAST likely to be found at the same trophic level in a food web?
(A) Cow and grasshopper.
(B) Fox and hawk.
(C) Rabbit and cow.
(D) Sheep and wolf.
(E) Toad and anteater.

53. In North America, the temperature range and length of growing season are similar in a prairie and a deciduous forest. Which of the following is the major determining factor as to whether the dominant community in a specific location will be forest or prairie?
(A) Soil type
(B) Fauna.
(C) Available moisture .
(D)Amount of sunlight.
(E) Latitude.

54. Which of the following would have the LEAST effect on the population density of a species?
(A) Predators.
(B) Competitors.
(C) Decomposers.
(D) Parasites.
(E) Nutrients

55. Biological control of harmful insects refers to
(A) Regularly scheduled burning of fields.
(B) The use of nonpersistent pesticides.
(C) The use of one organism to limit the growth of another.
(D) The use of herbicides.
(E) The use of biodegradable pesticides

56. Which of the following statements is true of the carbon cycle?
(A) The seasonal pulse in CO2 in the atmosphere is the result of increased numbers of animals born in spring.
(B) The burning of wood and fossil fuel takes CO2 from the atmosphere.
(C) Photosynthesis and respiration are responsible for major transformations of carbon.
(D) CO2 is returned to the atmosphere by photosynthesis.
(E) Assimilation of CO2 by plants is greater than the return of CO2 to the atmosphere from respiration, decomposition, and combustion

57. Which of the following is the best example of a population?
(A) A grouping of Douglas fir trees (Pseudotsuga menziesii) along the left bank of a Canadian river.
(B) The sum of all the toads of the species Bufo bufo found in North America.
(C) All the garter snakes of the subspecies Thamnophis sirtalis sirtalis.
(D) The living organisms inhabiting a wooded area in central Maryland in 2001.
(E) The organisms common to the chaparral.

58. The activity of nitrogen-fixing bacteria in the root nodules of leguminous plants results in all of the following EXCEPT:
(A) Fixed nitrogen for plant growth.
(B) Increased organic matter in the soil.
(C) Reduced organic carbon for bacterial growth.
(D) Decreased leaf growth.
(E) Increased nitrate in the soil.

Question 59-60:

In the mid-1990's six pairs of bald eagles from Alaska were released in southern Indiana. By the next year, four of these pairs had produced offspring, but embryos in the eggs of the other two pairs failed to develop. The first four pairs nested near a reservoir that provides water to surrounding communities, while the other two pairs nested beside a lake contaminated with industrial chemical,
including polychlorinated biphenyls (PCB's).

59. Which of the following hypotheses is LEAST likely to explain the failure of the two pairs to reproduce successfully?
(A) The birds in these pairs carried mutations that prevented their eggs from developing.
(B) Industrial activity near the nests may have disturbed the birds' care of their eggs.
(C) PCB's from the lake poisoned the embryos.
(D) The nesting area contained a virus or bacterium that adversely affected the birds.
(E) The climate in Indiana inhibited the development of the embryos.

60. Analysis of eggshell fragments showed higher toxin concentrations in the eggs of the bald eagles whose embryos failed to develop, than in those of the successful eagles. This result is most likely an example of
(A) Ecological succession.
(B) Biological magnification.
(C) Competitive exclusion.
(D) Industrial melanism.
(E) Biochemical cycles

61. Zygops rufitorquis, a slow-moving weevil, has the same markings as a flesh fly, a fast-flying insect that is difficult I for predators to catch. This is an example of which of the following biological phenomena?
(A) The founder principle.
(B) Allopatric speciation.
(C) Adaptive radiation.
(D) Directional selection.
(E) Mimicry.

62. Which of the following observations would provide the greatest support for a biologist's hypothesis that two populations of salamanders belong to one species?

(A) The two populations have similar colorations and arrangements of spots.
(B) The members of both populations feed on insect prey, but the insects are different.
(C) The two populations live in separate isolated but similar habitats.
(D) When the two members of the two populations interbreed, they produce fertile offspring.
(E) Fossils of early salamanders have been found near the present locations of the two populations

63. Which of the following is an example of primary succession?

(A) Soil formation in the crater of an extinct volcano.
(B) Growth of a jack pine forest after a major forest fire.
(C) Restoration of a tall grass prairie ecosystem on a former wheat field.
(D) Starfish colonizing a coral reef.
(E) Spruce trees growing on land after logging companies have clear-cut the original forest.

64. In a food pyramid, which of the following derives the most energy from the amount originally contained in plant material?
(A) A human drinking cow's milk
(B) A fox eating a rabbit
(C) A cow eating grass
(D) A sea gull eating fish
(E) A mountain lion eating a fox

65. Reducing the amount of runoff from feedlots and milking yards on a farm will result in which of the following?
(A) An increase in algal growth in lakes that receive the runoff
(B) An increase in the productivity of the farms animal stocks
(C) An increase in the water required to run the farm successfully
(D) A decrease in the total milk production of the farm
(E) A decrease in the eutrophication of lakes that receive the runoff

66. A parasite that is evolutionarily successful is one that.
(A) Kills its host.
(B) Has a well-developed digestive system.
(C) Is larger than its host.
(D) Inhabits the intestinal tract.
(E) Flourishes yet allow its host to survive.

67. A major role of certain bacteria in ecosystems is the conversion of.
(A) Nitrogen to ammonia
(B) Oxygen to ozone.
(C) Sodium to sodium chloride.
(D) Hydrogen to water.
(E) Calcium carbonate to carbon dioxide.

68. Most of the carbon on the Earth is found in rocks and has little direct effect on photosynthesis because.
(A) It circulates in the carbon cycle very slowly.
(B) It is readily available to the biosphere.
(C) The rocks weather readily to release the carbon.
(D) Only bicarbonate is used in photosynthesis.
(E) Carbon-containing minerals are completely insoluble.

69. Some harmless species resemble unrelated species that are poisonous or distasteful. This is a special case of which of the following?
(A) Mimicry.
(B) Divergent evolution.
(C) Allopathic speciation.
(D) Hardy-Weinberg equilibrium.
(E) Founder effect.

70. Which of the following factors that limit population size would be considered density-dependent?
(A) A drought.
(B) A tornado.
(C) A blizzard.
(D) A disease outbreak.
(E) An oil spill

Questions 71-74:

For a study on the environment, a group of students gathered samples of surface soil and any dead plant material covering it from locations around their school. They performed chemical soil tests including pH levels and measured the relative amounts of nitrogen (N), phosphorus (P), and potassium (K), extracted tiny animals, and cultured microorganisms. Their results are shown in the table below.

Sample	Location	pH	N	P	K	Animal	Abundance of Fungi and Bacteria	Depth of Covering Material
I	Beside tennis court	8	High	Low	High	3 species 9 organisms	Medium	0.50 cm
II	Wooded area	5	Low	Med.	Med.	8 species 40 organisms	High	2.00 cm
III	Near student parking lot	7	Low	Med.	Med.	4 species 45 organisms	Medium	0.50 cm
IV	Front lawn	7	High	High	High	1 species 2 organisms	Low	0.25 cm
V	Near trash dumpster	7	Med.	Med.	Low	None	Very low	None

71. Which of the sample areas shows the greatest diversity of animal species?
(A) I
(B) II
(C) III
(D) IV
(E) V

72. Which of the following variables shows the strongest positive correlation?
(A) Amount of nitrogen and number of animals.
(B) Depth of covering material and number of animals.
(C) Depth of covering material and abundance of fungi and bacteria.
(D) Number of organisms and number of species.
(E) Potassium and pH

73. Which area shows characteristics consistent with the recent application of a balanced garden fertilizer?
(A) I
(B) II
(C) III
(D) IV
(E) V

74. Which sample is most likely to exhibit a relatively constant soil temperature over the course of a summer day?
(A) I
(B) II
(C) III
(D) IV
(E) V

Questions 75-78:

The graphs below show population growth characteristics of either a single species (graphs I and II) or the interaction between two species (graphs III and IV).

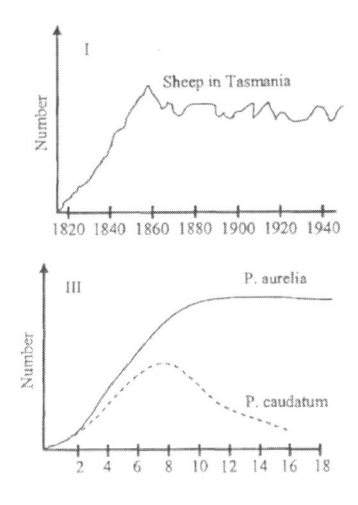

75. In which of the following graphs is a species growing according to the logistic equation and stabilizing near the carrying capacity?
(A) I only.
(B) III only.
(C) I and II only.
(D) I and III only.
(E) III and IV only

76. A species responding to interspecific competition is shown in which of the following graphs?
(A) I only
(B) II only
(C) III only
(D) N only
(E) I and III only

77. Predator-prey interactions are illustrated in which of the following graphs?
(A) I only.
(B) II only.
(C) III only.
(D) IV only.
(E) II and IV only

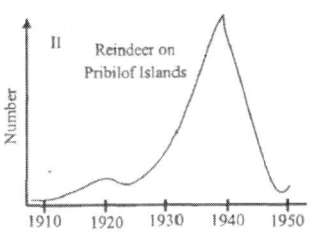

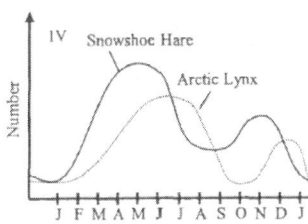

78. Which of the following graphs most likely illustrates a species that greatly exceeded its carrying capacity?
(A) II only.
(B) III only.
(C) IV only.
(D) I and III only.
(E) I, II, and IV only

79. Which of the following is a density-independent factor?
(A) Disease
(B) Famine
(C) Floods
(D) Predation
(E) Increase in toxins in the environment

(C) Earthquakes
(D) Tsunamis
(E) Naturally occurring fires

80. If the food chain shown here is controlled from the *bottom up*, what will happen if human activity results in the removal of hawks from the environment?

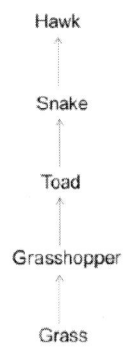

Hawk
↑
Snake
↑
Toad
↑
Grasshopper
↑
Grass

(A) Snakes, toads, grasshoppers, and grass will *increase* in abundance.
(B) Snakes, toads, grasshoppers, and grass will *decrease* in abundance
(C) Snakes and grasshoppers will *decrease* in abundance; toads and grass will *increase* in abundance.
(D) Snakes and grasshoppers will *increase* in abundance; toads and grass will *decrease* in abundance.
(E) The abundance of snakes, toads, grasshoppers, and grass will not change

81. Which of the following is the best example of a biome?
(A) A rocky cave
(B) A dry riverbed
(C) An expansive deciduous forest
(D) A tern nesting area and the terns that inhabit it
(E) The fish that inhabit the area around a coral reef

82. All of the following are density-independent factors EXCEPT
(A) Floods
(B) Famine

83. Which of the following constitutes a likely food chain?
(A) Squid-small fish-algae-orca whales-copepods
(B) Copepods-squid-small fish-algae-orca whales
(C) Algae-copepods-small fish-squid-orca whales
(D) Copepods-algae-squid-small fish-orca whales
(E) Algae-small fish-squid-copepods-orca whales

84. Characteristics of the arctic tundra biome include which of the following?
  I.   Lichens growing on bare rock
  II. High levels of precipitation
  III. Permafrost

(A) I only
(B) III only
(C) I and II only
(D) I and III only
(E) I, II, and III

85. Deep-ocean communities (abyssal zone) are dimly lit and have few photosynthetic organisms. Which of the following is true of these areas?
(A) Primary productivity is high
(B) Level of dissolved oxygen are low
(C) Contain most of the organisms in the oceans
(D) High concentration of algae
(E) High concentration of green plants

86. The world human population today can best be described as
(A) Fluctuating around the carrying capacity
(B) At equilibrium
(C) Growing arithmetically
(D) Growing exponentially
(E) Growing very slowly

87. An organism's niche is :
  (A) The range of temperatures that the organism needs to survive
  (B) A full description of the place an organism lives

(C) The range of physical and biological conditions in which an organism lives and the way it obtains what it needs to survive and reproduce
(D) All the physical factors in the organism's environment
(E) All the biological factors in the organism's environment

88. Which of the following statements best describes "true-breeding" plants?
(A) When one of these plants self-pollinates, all of its offspring are fertile.
(B) When two individuals of the same phenotype are mated, their offspring will all have that phenotype.
(C) All of the organisms in the F1 generation are heterozygous.
(D) The plants always reproduce asexually
(E) The plants produce a significantly large number of offspring.

89. The amount of energy produced by primary producers is always:

(A) equal to the amount of solar energy they absorb.
(B) less than the amount of solar energy they absorb.
(C) greater than the amount of solar energy they absorb.
(D) equal to, less than, or greater than the amount of solar energy they absorb, depending on the specific ecosystem they inhabit.
(E) higher in aquatic environments than in terrestrial environments.

90. In ruminant animals such as cows, bacteria inhabit the digestive tract and aid in the digestion of grasses. In this situation, the relationship between the bacteria and the cow is an example of.
(A) Parasitism.
(B) Saprophytism.
(C) Competition.
(D) Mutualism.
(E) Predation.

91. A plot of soil was completely stripped of all of its vegetation and left undisturbed by humans. The first plants to become the dominant vegetation will probably be.
(A) Annual herbs.
(B) Lichens.
(C) Shrubs.
(D) Deciduous trees.
(E) Evergreens.

92. Which of the following biomes contains the greatest biodiversity?
(A) Tundra
(B) Chaparral
(C) Coral reef
(D) Benthic ocean
(E) Temperate deciduous forest

93. Which of the following is LEAST likely to be a threat to the survival of a species?
(A) Environmental pollution.
(B) Genetic homogeneity.
(C) Random mating.
(D) Reduction of habitat.
(E) Interspecific competition.

94. At the boundary between two major layers of rock in Earth's surface-the Cretaceous and Tertiary-geologists have found a thin layer of rock enriched in iridium, an element that is very rare on Earth. This is part of the evidence suggesting that dinosaurs became extinct because of
(A) the impact of a meteor
(B) brain function that was inferior to mammals'
(C) a climate change that brought freezing temperatures to the Northern Hemisphere
(D) extensive flooding from melting ice caps
(E) a disease epidemic caused by unusual Microorganisms

95. The most dangerous aspect of the use of the pesticide DDT is that it
(A) kills plants as well as insects
(B) accumulates in higher trophic levels
(C) leaches nitrogen from the soil
(D) depletes the ozone layer
(E) can be used as food by harmful bacteria

96. Two animal populations are considered to be of the same species if their members
    (A) Eat the same food
    (B) Can live in similar ecological niches
    (C) Can interbreed to produce live, fertile offspring
    (D) interbreeded within the same geographic area
    (E) migrate to new locations at the same time of the year

97. Inbreeding tends to produce
    (A) An increase in the frequency of certain characteristics
    (B) Offspring that are larger than normal
    (C) Heterozygous offspring
    (D) Increased strength and vigor in the offspring
    (E) Greater genetic diversity in the offspring

98. The major ecological role of heterotrophs is to
    (A) Recycle carbon and oxygen
    (B) Control soil erosion
    (C) Provide organic compounds for autotrophs
    (D) Purify water
    (E) Act as a primary producer

99. Which of the following biomes contain the greatest diversity of species?
    (A) Temperate forest
    (B) Temperate grassland
    (C) Boreal taiga
    (D) Tropical savanna
    (E) Tropical rain forest

100. The largest population of omnivores can be supported if they secure their food predominantly from
(A) Primary producers
(B) Primary consumers
(C) Secondary consumers
(D) Decomposers
(E) Other omnivores

101. All of the following processes occur as part of the carbon cycle EXCEPT
(A) Organic decay
(B) Forest fires
(C) Photosynthesis
(D) Respiration
(E) Transpiration

102. Characteristics of the arctic tundra biome include which of the following?
    I. Long, cold winters
    II. Coniferous trees as the dominant species
    III. High levels of precipitation
(A) I only
(B) III only
(C) I and II only
(D) II and III only
(E) I, II, and III

103. A trophic level within an ecosystem is best defined by the
(A) Total chemical energy contained in nutrients within the ecosystem
(B) Total available energy captured by photosynthesis within an ecosystem
(C) Amount of pollution within the ecosystem
(D) Main source of nutrition of the organisms within it
(E) Density of the population relative to the carrying capacity of the environment

104. All of the following are population characteristics EXCEPT
(A) Number of individuals
(B) Phenotype
(C) Sex ratio
(D) Age distribution
(E) Death rate

105. The prediction that the Earth's climate will warm in the next 100 years is based on which of the following observations?
I. Dust and particles are increasing in the upper atmosphere.
II. Carbon dioxide is increasing in the atmosphere.
III. Methane gas is increasing in the atmosphere
(A) I only
(B) II only
(C) III only
(D) I and II only
(E) II and III only

106. Stream and river ecosystems differ from other aquatic ecosystems because streams and rivers
(A) move continuously in one direction and have a nutrient content that is dependent on location
(B) support a greater diversity of aquatic plants
(C) have highly variable salinity
(D) include the greatest biodiversity of all ecosystems because of the fluctuating water levels
(E) support the largest stationary plankton communities

107. According to most scientific theories of the origin of Life, the first organisms were
(A) eukaryotic
(B) parasitic
(C) Aerobic
(D) Anaerobic
(E) pathogenic

108. Which of the following does NOT refer primarily to a relationship between members of different species?
(A) Mutualism
(B) Hibernation
(C) Parasitism
(D) Commensalism
(E) Predation

Answers:

1. D
2. A
3. C
4. D
5. B
6. E
7. B
8. D
9. D
10. B
11. B
12. B
13. ......
14. ....
15. D
16. D
17. C
18. E
19. A
20. C
21. A
22. B
23. C
24. A
25. A
26. C
27. A
28. D
29. D
30. A
31. D
32. C
33. C
34. E
35. D
36. D
37. D
38. B
39. E
40. C
41. C
42. D
43. C
44. B
45. A
46. D
47. E
48. D
49. ....
50. D
51. A
52. D
53. E
54. C
55. C
56. C
57. A
58. D
59. E
60. B
61. E
62. D
63. A
64. C
65. E
66. E
67. A
68. A
69. A
70. D
71. B
72. C
73. D
74. C
75. A
76. C
77. D
78. A
79. C

80.D
81.C
82.B
83.C
84.B
85.B
86.D
87.C
88.B
89.B
90.D
91.A
92……….
93.C
94.A
95.B
96.C
97.A
98.A
99.E
100.A
101.E
102.A
103.A
104.B
105.E
106.A
107.D
108.B

Genetics

1. Which of the following crosses is a testcross?
(A) AA x AA
(B) AA X Aa
(C) Aa x Aa
(D) A_ x aa
(E) aa x aa

2. A rancher bought a bull guaranteed not to have a certain unwanted recessive allele of an autosomal gene. He crossed the bull to cows who were homozygous for the unwanted allele, with the result that 3 of the offspring were normal and 2 had the undesired trait. Which of the following is the best conclusion to be drawn from this result?

(A) The bull is homozygous dominant for the unwanted allele.
(B) The bull is homozygous recessive for the unwanted allele.
(C) The cows are really heterozygous for the unwanted allele.
(D) It is not possible for selective breeding to determine the genotype of an animal, so the original guarantee was unreasonable.
(E) The rancher was cheated; the bull is heterozygous for the unwanted allele

3. A certain characteristic in human is inherited as an autosomal recessive trait . if a man with the trait and a woman without it have three sons without the trait, which of the following can be concluded ?
(A) The children are heterozygous for the trait
(B) The woman is homozygous recessive for the trait
(C) The man is heterozygous for the trait
(D) The fourth child will have the trait
(E) The trait is sex-linked

4. In a certain plant species, the trait tall T is dominant to dwarf t and the color red R is dominant to white r .To determine whether a particular tall red plant is heterozygous or homozygous for both characteristics , the plant would be best crossed with which of the following?
(A) TTRR
(B) TtRr
(C) ttRR
(D) TTrr
(E) ttrr

5. Which of the following are the genotypes of a couple that have 4 children, each with a different blood type?
(A) AA and Bi
(B) AB and Bi
(C) Ai and AB
(D) Ai and Bi
(E) AB and ii

Questions 6-10 :

(A) Meiosis
(B) Mitosis
(C) Fertilization
(D) Mutation
(E) Crossing-over

6. Process by which the number of chromosomes is reduced to the half
7. Process by which the number of chromosomes is restored
8. Process by which the number of chromosomes is kept constant in all the cells of an organism
9. Process by which chromosomes exchange materials
10. Process by which DNA changes in composition

11. A and a are alleles of one gene, and B and b are alleles of another gene. The two genes are not linked. If a parent has the genotype AaBb , which gamete types could be produced?
(A) AB only
(B) Aa and Bb only
(C) AB and ab only
(D) Ab and aB only
(E) AB, Ab, aB, ab

12. In sheep, white wool is due to single dominant allele and black wool is due to recessive allele. Two sheep with white wool are mated and produce a lamb with black wool. If they produce another lamb, what is the probability that it will have white wool?
(A) 0%
(B) 25%
(C) 50%
(D) 75%
(E) 100%

13. Turner's Syndrome (XO) is a chromosomal disorder that can be diagnosed by
(A) Pedigree analysis
(B) Biochemical analysis
(C) Punnett square analysis
(D) Karyotyping
(E) Blood type analysis

Questions 14-16 :

In cross the gene for leaf color has two alleles. The allele for purple leaf color (B) is dominant to that for green leaf color (b). the following data were gathered for three separate crosses.

	Parents		offspring
Cross	Female	Male	
I	Purple X	Purple	45 Purple
			14 Green
II	Purple X	Green	60 Purple
			0 Green
III	Purple X	Green	31 Purple
			30 Green

14. Based on the data above, the genotype of the parents in cross I are correctly represented by which of the following?
(A) Bb X bb
(B) Bb X Bb
(C) BB X bb
(D) BB X Bb
(E) BB X BB

15. A cross between any two of the offspring of cross II would yield offspring with a leaf color ratio similar to that seen in cross
(A) I only
(B) II only
(C) III only
(D) I or II only
(E) II or III only

16. The offspring with purple leaves in cross III are expected to be which of the following genotypes ?
(A) 100% BB
(B) 100% Bb
(C) 67% BB and 33% Bb
(D) 50% BB and 50% Bb
(E) 33% BB and 67% Bb

17. If a trait is controlled by a single gene pair, then the genotype of an individual carrying identical alleles for that trait is referred to as
(A) Hybrid
(B) Dominant
(C) Recessive
(D) Haploid
(E) Homozygous

18. Huntington's disease is a degenerative disorder of the nervous system that follows an inheritance pattern of autosomal dominance. What is the probability that a child will inherit Huntington's disease if one of the parents has an allele for the disease?
(A) 0%
(B) 25%
(C) 50%
(D) 75%
(E) 100%

19. Pattern baldness is a sex-linked recessive trait characterized by hair loss near the hairline and at the crown of the head. If a woman whose father is bald and a man who is bald have a son, what is the probability that the son will inherit the allele for pattern baldness? Assume that the woman's mother does not carry the allele for pattern baldness.
(A) 0%
(B) 25%
(C) 50%
(D) 75%
(E) 100%

20. A testcross is used to determine the genotype of a plant showing the dominant tall trait. Which of the following probably shows that the plant is heterozygous?
   I. All the offspring show the dominant trait.
   II. All of the offspring show the recessive trait
   III. Some of the offspring are tall.
   IV. None of the offspring are short.
(A) I only.
(B) II only.
(C) III only.
(D) IV only.
(E) III and IV

21. Chromosomal mutations include all of the following EXCEPT
(A) Deletion
(B) Duplication
(C) Inversion
(D) Translocation
(E) Synapsis

22. Two mature plants that are each 12 centimeters in height are crossed and produce offspring ranging from 4 to 18 centimeters in height when mature. Of the following, which is most likely explanation for these results?
(A) Tallness is dominant over shortness
(B) Multiple genes affect heights in plants
(C) Height is a sex-linked trait in plants
(D) Non-disjunction has occurred
(E) A mutation has occurred

23. A particular characteristic in human is inherited as an autosomal recessive trait . if a man with the trait and a woman without it have three sons without the trait, which of the following can be concluded ?

(A) The children are heterozygous for the trait
(B) The woman is homozygous recessive for the trait
(C) The man is heterozygous for the trait
(D) The fourth child will have the trait
(E) The trait is sex-linked

	i	I^B
I^A	¹A	²AB
I^B	³B	⁴B
i	⁵O	⁶O

24.

The numbered boxes in the table above show four human blood types based on various pairings of the three alleles that code for blood type: I^A, I^B and i. The alleles I^A and I^B are co-dominant. An incorrect blood type is shown in which box or boxes?
(A) 1 and 2
(B) 3
(C) 4 and 5
(D) 6
(E) 3 and 6

25. If two parents are carriers of the same allele for a recessive trait and their first five children exhibit the dominant phenotype, the probability that their next child will exhibit the recessive phenotype 15
(A) 0
(B) ¼
(C) ½
(D) ¾
(E) 1

26. What percentage of offspring from the cross BbTT x bbTt would be expected to have the genotype BbTt?
(A) ¾
(B) ½
(C) ¼
(D) 1/8
(E) 1/16

27. A researcher has a black guinea pig and wishes to determine if it carries a recessive allele for white hair. Both of the guinea pigs parents are black. Which of the following would be the best method for the researcher to use?
(A) Mate the guinea pig with another black guinea pig and look for white offspring
(B) Look for white hairs on the guinea pig.
(C) Mate the guinea pig with a white guinea pig and look for white offspring.
(D) Observe the chromosomes of a hair cell from a black hair
(E) See if the guinea pig has any white siblings

Questions 28-29 refer to the following.

(A) 2
(B) 4
(C) 16
(D) 25
(E) 50

28. The expected percentage of offspring with the recessive phenotype from a cross between two individuals heterozygous for a particular trait

29. The number of different phenotypes possible for the progeny of the cross AaBb x AaBb, where A and B exhibit simple dominance

30. A cross between two individuals results in a ratio of 9:3:3:1 for four possible phenotypes. This is an example of a
(A) dihybrid cross.
(B) monohybrid cross.
(C) testcross.
(D) none of these.
(E) Incomplete dominance

31. True statements about linked genes include which of the following?
I. The alleles for linked genes may recombine due to crossing over.
II. Linked genes are on the same chromosome.
III. Linked genes occur only on the sex chromosome.
(A) I only.
(B) II only.
(C) III only.
(D) I and II only.
(E) I, II, and III.

Question 32-36:

A study of a species of flowering plant indicated that tall (T) is dominant over dwarf (t). It was also found that in this species, plants homozygous for the R allele have red flowers, plants homozygous for the r allele have white flowers, and plants heterozygous for the allele have pink flowers.

32. The traits under study are inherited according to which of the following patterns?
(A) Complete dominance for both traits.
(B) Incomplete dominance for both traits.
(C) Incomplete dominance for one trait and complete dominance for the other trait.
(D) Sex linkage in the gene for height and complete dominance for color.
(E) Sex linkage in the color gene and complete dominance for height.

33. A white-flowered plant homozygous for tallness is crossed with a red-flowered dwarf plant. Which of the following gives the expected genotype and phenotype for the first generation?
(A) ttRr- dwarf, pink.
(B) ttrr- dwarf, white.
(C) Ttrr- tall, red.
(D) TtRr- tall, pink.
(E) TTrr- tall, pink.

34. If two plants of genotypes ttRr and TtRR are crossed and no mutations occur, what percent of the offspring is expected to be dwarf white-flowered plants?

(A) 0%
(B) 25%
(C) 50%
(D) 75%
(E) 100%

35. If pollen from a plant heterozygous for height is used to fertilize a dwarf plant, which of the following would be the expected ratios of the offspring?
(A) All tall.
(B) All dwarf.
(C) ¼ tall : ¾ dwarf.
(D) ½ tall: ½ dwarf.
(E) All of intermediate height.

36. If two pink-flowered plants are crossed, the expected percentage of pink-flowering plants in the first generation is.
(A) 100%
(B) 75%
(C) 50%
(D) 25%
(E) 0%

37. In the inheritance of human blood groups, it is known that the alleles for blood types A and B are dominant to the allele for type O, and that the alleles for types A and B are codominant. Children of two parents of blood type O are most likely to be.
(A) Type O only.
(B) Any type but O.
(C) Types A or B only.
(D) Type AB only.
(E) Any one of the four types, A, B, AB, or O.

Questions 38-41 :

Refer to the pedigree shown below that illustrates the transmission of trait called albinism, the lack of pigmentation. For **the** family tree shown in this pedigree, the trait has only two alleles. A is dominant and a is recessive

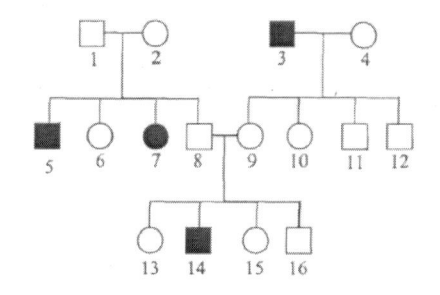

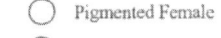

37. According to the pedigree, one can correctly conclude that
    (A) Most of the family members are albino.
    (B) Parents who are normally pigmented can have a child who is albino.
    (C) Parents who are both albino can have a normally pigmented child.
    (D) Albinism is virally transmitted.
    (E) Albino individuals can have normally pigmented brothers but not normally pigmented sisters

39. The genotype of a person who exhibits albinism is correctly expressed by
    (A) AA only.
    (B) Aa only.
    (C) aa only.
    (D) Aa or aa.
    (E) AA or Aa.

40. The genotypes of individuals 1 and 2, respectively, are
    (A) AA and Aa.
    (B) Aa and Aa.
    (C) Aa and aa.
    (D) AA and aa.
    (E) Not determinable from the data

41. If individuals 8 and 9 have another child, the chance that this child will exhibit albinism is.
    (A) 0%
    (B) 25%
    (C) 50%
    (D) 75%
    (E) 100%

42. If an evergreen variety of wood fern is crossed with a nearby deciduous variety of wood fern, all the offspring are deciduous. This evidence suggests that the inheritance of this trait is most likely a case of.
    (A) Sex-linked inheritance.
    (B) Multiple allelic inheritance.
    (C) Simple dominance.
    (D) Codominance.
    (E) Mutation.

43. A man in his early twenties learns that his father has been diagnosed with Huntington disease. This rare disease is caused by a dominant allele and usually does not manifest itself with middle age. There is no history of the disease in the young man's mother's family. What is the probability that the young man will develop the symptoms of the disease when he is older?

    (A) 0%
    (B) 25%
    (C) 50%
    (D) 66%
    (E) 75%

44. Which of the following are the genotypes of a couple that have four children, each with a different blood type?
(A) AA and BO
(B) AB and BO
(C) AO and AB
(D) AO and BO
(E) AB and OO

45. What percentage of offspring from the cross BbTI x bbTt would be expected to have the genotype BbTt?
(A) ¾
(B) ½
(C) ¼
(D) 1/8
(E) 1/16

46. Which of the following statements best describes "true-breeding" plants?

(A) When one of these plants self-pollinates, all of its offspring are fertile.
(B) When two individuals of the same phenotype are mated, their offspring will all have that phenotype.
(C) All of the organisms in the F1 generation are heterozygous.
(D) The plants always reproduce asexually
(E) The plants produce a significantly large number of offspring .

47. An animal breeder notices that one breeding pair nearly always produces at least one albino per litter, with a ratio of 1 albino to 3 normally pigmented animals. All the albinos from this breeding pair are males. Which of the following is the most likely mode of inheritance for this type of albinism?

(A) Autosomal recessive.
(B) Autosomal dominant.
(C) Autosomal lethal.
(D) Sex-linked dominant.
(E) Sex-linked recessive

48. Some genes are carried only on the Y chromosome. A man carrying genes for a particular trait on this chromosome will normally transmit the trait to.
(A) One-half of his sons.
(B) One-half of his daughters.
(C) All of his daughters.
(D) All of his sons.
(E) All of his children.

49. What type of mutation involves the addition or deletion of nucleotides?
    (A) Nonsense
    (B) Missense
    (C) Silent
    (D) Frameshift
    (E) Inversion

50. If a trait is controlled by a single gene pair, then the genotype of an individual carrying identical alleles for that trait is referred to as.
(A) Hybrid.
(B) Dominant
(C) Recessive.
(D) Haploid.
(E) Homozygous.

51. A particular characteristic in humans is inherited as an autosomal recessive trait. If a man with the trait and a woman without it have three sons without the trait, which of the following can be concluded?
(A) The children are heterozygous for the trait.
(B) The woman is homozygous recessive for the trait.
(C) The man is heterozygous for the trait.
(D) The fourth child will have the trait.
(E) The trait is sex-linked.

52. A population of mice with coat colors ranging from black to white, including all intermediate shades, is introduced into a habitat primarily composed of black rocks in which there are a number of aerial predators. After several generations, which of the following will most likely be true of the coat color in this population of mice?
(A) Coat color will revert to the wild type
(B) The ratio of black coat color to white coat color will be 3:1
(C) The black coat color will disappear.
(D) The population will become dimorphic for coat color.
(E) The average coat color will become darker

53. In sheep, white wool is due to a single dominant allele and black wool is due to the recessive allele. Two sheep with white wool are mated and produce a lamb with black wool. If they produce another lamb, what is the probability that it will have white wool?
(A) 0%
(B) 25%
(C) 50%
(D) 75%
(E) 100%

Questions 54-55:

A Student repeated one of Mendel's experiments. A plant having green pods was self-fertilized and produced a first generation consisting of 793 plants with green pods and 275 with yellow pods

54. Approximately how many of the 793 green-pod plants would be expected to be homozygous for pod color?
(A) 0
(B) 100
(C) 250
(D) 500
(E) 793

55. If the original plant is fertilized by a yellow-pod plant, what proportion of the offspring can be expected to be Yellew-pod plants?
(A) 0
(B) 1/4
(C) 1/2
(D) 3/4
(E) 1

56. Why are frame-shift mutations particularly dangerous?
(A) They shorten the length of chromosomes.
(B) No other mutation changes phenotypes.
(C) They prevent transcription from occurring.
(D) They affect all codons following the mutation.
(E) Future offspring will be sterile

57. In the accompanying table, which amino acid sequence would most likely be determined by a section of a DNA molecule with the base sequence C-C-G-T- C-T-A-C-C

Amino Acid	mRNA Codon
Alanine	GGC
Arginine	AGA
Leucine	CUA
Tryptophan	UGG

(A) Alanine- arginine - tryptophan
(B) Alanine- arginine - leucine
(C) Arginine -leucine - tryptophan
(D) Arginine- alanine - leucine
(E) Tryptophan - leucine – arginine

58. Which of the following concepts did Mendel describe?
I. Dominant/recessive inheritance.
II. Independent assortment.
III. Segregation of characteristics.

(A) I only.
(B) II only.
(C) III only.
(D) I and II only.
(E) I, II, and III.

59. A botanist wants to breed a new variety of daisy with orange flowers. She crosses a yellow variety with a red variety.
She knows that the daisy with yellow petals contains a dominant yellow petal allele and a recessive white petal allele.
In which scenario is it possible to obtain an orange flower?
    (A) Red petals have incomplete dominance to yellow petals and are dominant to white petals.
    (B) Red petals have incomplete dominance to white petals and are recessive to yellow petals.
    (C) Red petals are dominant to yellow petals and white petals.
    (D) Red petals are dominant to yellow petals and co-dominant to white petals.
    (E) Red petals are recessive to yellow petals and dominant to white petals

60. Which of the following result(s) in an inherited change?
  I. Gene mutation
  II. Chromosomal aberration
  III. Mineral deficiency

(A) I only
(B) II only
(C) III only
(D) I and II only
(E) I and III only

Questions 61-63:

The gene for acertain protein has been isolated and sequenced from five different species. During their evolution from a common ancestor. these species have undergone only single-nucleotide mutations. A partial

  I. 3'...AGTAC...5'
  II. 3'...AGTTC...5'
  III. 3'...AGTAT...5'
  IV. 3'...TGTTC...5'
  V. 3'...ACTTC...5'

61. The sequence 5' ... UGAAG ... 3' would most likely represent an RNA sequence transcribed from which-of the following species?

(A) I
(B) II
(C) III
(D) IV
(E) V

62. Which of the species would require the fewest point mutations in the original sequence in order to give rise to the new sequence 3'... GGTAT ... 5'?

(A) I
(B) II
(C) III
(D) IV
(E) V

63. Which is most likely to be the oldest species if 3'... AGAAC ... 5' were the partial DNA sequence of the common ancestor of the group?
(A) I
(B) II
(C) III
(D) IV
(E) V

Answers:

1. D
2.

Human Body

1. Two hormones produced by hypothalamus are
   (A) LH and FSH.
   (B) ADH and oxytocin.
   (C) ACTH and TSH.
   (D) Cortisol and GH
   (E) Oxytocin and prolactin

2. If blood progesterone level is very low, which of the following will **not** occur?
   (A) Ovulation
   (B) Maintenance of thickened endometrium during pregnancy
   (C) Contraction of myometrium at child birth
   (D) Production of milk
   (E) Menstruation

3. The hormone estrogen does which of the following?
   I. It controls secondary sexual characteristics
   II. It inhibits the production of some hormones by the anterior pituitary
   III. It is present in females at variable levels

   (A) I only
   (B) II only
   (C) I and II only
   (D) II and III only
   (E) I, II, and III

4. At the neuromuscular junction, which of the following passes from the nerve cell to the muscle cell?
   (A) An electrical signal
   (B) A chemical signal
   (C) A magnetic signal
   (D) An axon
   (E) A synapse

5. The number of white blood cells in the human circulatory system is most directly affected by the
   (A) Presence or absence of infective agents in the blood
   (B) Altitude at which the individual lives
   (C) Amount of iron in the individual's diet
   (D) Amount of hemoglobin manufactured by the body
   (E) Sex of the individual

6. Which of the following is NOT a function of the placenta in human beings?
   (A) Conveying nutrients from the mother to the fetus.
   (B) Conveying CO_2, H_2O, and urea from the fetus to the mother
   (C) Conveying O_2 from the mother to the fetus.
   (D) Conveying nerve impulses from the mother to the fetus.
   (E) Serving as endocrine organ during pregnancy

7. A man and a woman have blood types A and B, respectively. Their first child had blood type AB, and the second child had blood type O. What correct prediction can be made about the blood types of subsequent children?
   (A) Half will have blood type AB and half will have blood type O.
   (B) They will have blood type A and B only.
   (C) Each child has an equal chance of having blood type A, B, AB, or O.
   (D) Any blood type is possible, but A and B are much more likely.
   (E) None of the children will have blood type A.

8. Villi of the small intestine and alveoli of the lung are alike in all of the following ways EXCEPT.
   (A) They increase the surface area for exchange of materials.
   (B) They have a thin layer of epithelial tissue.
   (C) They have extensive blood vessels
   (D) They are extremely numerous
   (E) They secrete a high volume of enzymes

9. Which of the following could explain the fact that a woman whose ovulation is normal may be infertile?
I. Her fallopian tubes are blocked.
II. Large quantities of luteinizing hormone. LH, are released just prior to ovulation.
III. Sperm movement is inhibited by an incompatible pH in the fluids of the vagina or uterus.
(A) I only.
(B) II only.
(C) I and III only.
(D) II and III only.
(E) I, II, and III

10. The exchange of O_2 and CO_2 between blood and air in the lungs occurs through the process of
(A) Diffusion
(B) Osmosis
(C) Secretion
(D) Active transport
(E) Pinocytosis

11. One effect of increasing the concentration of antidiuretic hormone (ADH) is to
(A) Reduce the permeability to water in the loop of Henle
(B) Reduce the permeability to water of the collecting ducts
(C) Reduce the blood volume.
(D) Increase the volume and output of urine.
(E) Increase the concentration and decrease the volume of urine.

12. Which of the following statements about temperature regulation in human living in hot environments is correct?
(A) Perspiration insulates the body and prevents heat loss.
(B) Evaporation of perspiration cools the surface of the skin.
(C) Blood is shunted from the head region to the body cavity.
(D) Blood is more likely to travel near the long bones than near the skin.
(E) Goose bumps cool by decreasing the surface area of the skin.

Questions 13-16 :
(A) Growth hormone
(B) Oxytocin
(C) Progesterone
(D) Aldosterone
(E) Glucagon

13. . Increases uterine contractions during child birth
14. . Stimulates the release of glucose to the blood
15. . Induces water reabsorption in the kidney
16. . Prepares the uterus for implantation of the fertilized egg

17. Excessive acid in the stomach can result in a hole in the wall of the organ. What is this hole called?
(A) Tumor
(B) Cancer
(C) Boil
(D) Ulcer
(E) Hemorrhoid

Questions 18-20 :

refer to the following diagrams showing the stages of cleavage

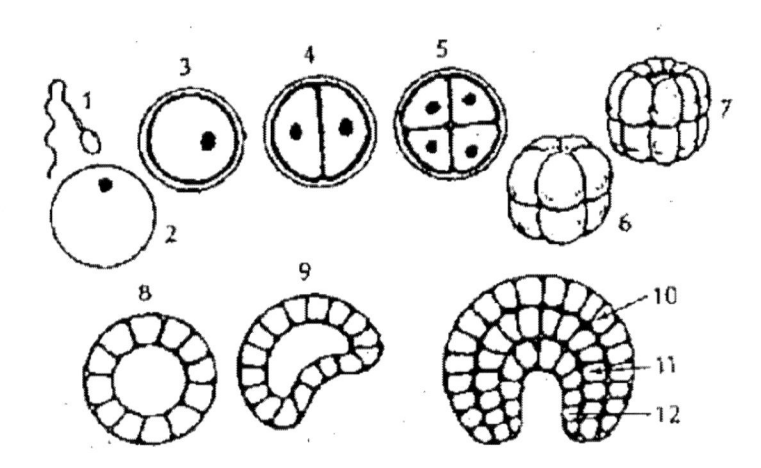

18. The first cell to contain the diploid number of chromosomes is
(A)2
(B) 3
(C)4
(D) 6
(E) 9

19. Which layer differentiates into the nervous system?
(A)6
(B) 7
(C)8
(D)9
(E) 10

20. Which Of the following, which is a gamete containing stored food?
(A)1
(B)2
(C)3
(D)8
(E) 9

21. A female gamete con taining the monoploid (haploid) number of chromosomes is
(A)2
(B)3
(C)4
(D)5
(E) 8

22. Which is the first cell to undergo mitotic division?
(A) 3
B) 4
(C) 5
(D) 6
(E) 8

23. In general, mammals show an inverse relationship between heart rate and body size. Which of the following graphs best indicates this relationship?

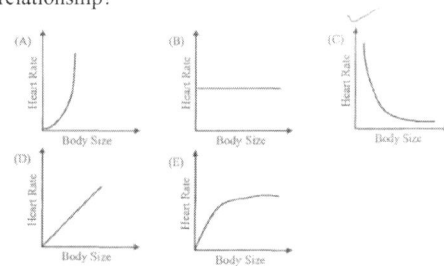

24. The number of white blood cells in the human circulatory system is most directly affected by the
(A) Presence or absence of infective agents in the blood
(B) Altitude at which the individual lives
(C) Amount of iron in the individual's diet
(D) Amount of hemoglobin manufactured by the body
(E) Sex of the individual

25. Which of the following is NOT a function of the placenta in human beings?
(A) Conveying nutrients from the mother to the fetus.
(B) Conveying CO_2, H_2O, and urea from the fetus to the moilier
(C) Conveying O_2 from the mother to the fetus.
(D) Conveying nerve impulses from the mother to the fetus.
(E) Serving as endocrine organ during pregnancy

26. Coffee contains caffeine, which inhibits the secretion of antidiuretic hormone (ADH). After coffee is consumed, the kidney produces
(A) A larger than normal volume of concentrated urine.
(B) A larger the normal volume of dilute urine.
(C) A smaller than normal volume of dilute urine.
(D) Salts to replace those that were eliminated.
(E) Diuretic hormone (DH) to counteract the effect of caffeine.

27. Sexual reproduction is beneficial to species because it
(A) Makes more efficient use of energy
(B) Increases genetic variability
(C) Brings organisms together for reproduction
(D) Keeps the species constant despite environmental changes
(E) Promotes interbreeding of different species

28. The protozoan that causes malaria in humans is
(A) An autotroph
(B) An herbivore
(C) A carnivore
(D) A scavenger
(E) A parasite

29. Tendons connect _____ to _____ ; ligaments connect _____ to
(A) bone to bone; bone to muscle
(B) bone to muscle; bone to bone
(C) bone to bone; muscle to muscle
(D) muscle to muscle; bone to bone
(E) ligaments to bone; tendons to bones

Questions 30-32 :

In an experiment, equal doses of a certain hormone marked with a harmless radioactive label were injected into several rats. Periodically thereafter, the amolmt of rad.loacuvity in various tissues (Figure A), and in subcellular locations of the eventual target cells for the hormone (Figure B) was measured

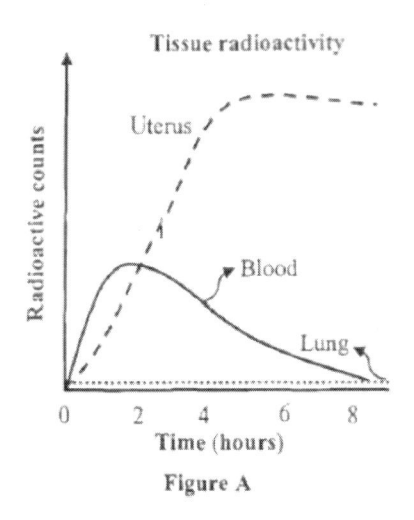

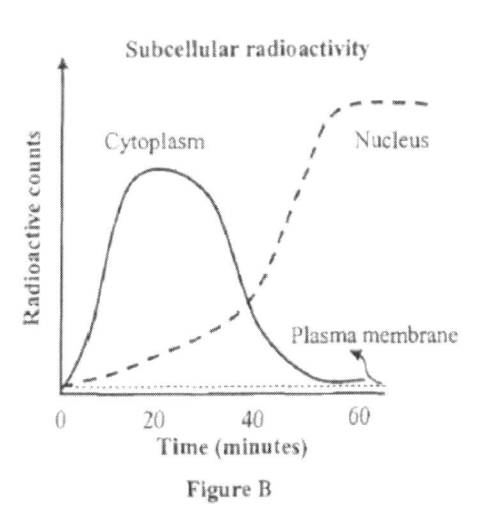

Figure A: Tissue radioactivity — Radioactive counts vs Time (hours), showing Uterus, Blood, Lung

Figure B: Subcellular radioactivity — Radioactive counts vs Time (minutes), showing Cytoplasm, Nucleus, Plasma membrane

30. Based on the data in figure A, which of the following is a reasonable conclusion?
(A) Uterine cells lack receptors for .this hormone.
(B) The most likely target of this hormone is the uterus.
(C) The lung is the most likely target tissue for this hormone.
(D) The hormone is probably not transported via the blood to the target cells.
(E) The hormone regulates the glucose level within the target cells.

31. Which of the following is the most likely mechanism of action for this hormone?
(A) The hormone binds tightly to the plasma membrane
(B) The hormone moves through the nucleus on its way to the cytoplasm
(C) The hormone binds to a cytoplasmic receptor and is then transported into the nucleus
(D) The hormone enters cells through chloride ion channels
(E) The hormone utilizes active transport to enter the cell

32. The hormone is most likely.
(A) Insulin.
(B) Norepinephrine.
(C) Antidiuretic hormone (ADH).
(D) Estrogen.
(E) Indolacetic acid (auxin)

Questions 33- 36:
Refer to this graph of an impulse passing across a neuron

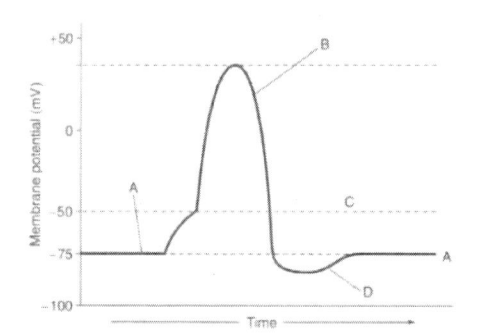

33. The impulse is passing
34. The sodium-potassium pump is responsible for pumping ions across the membrane
35. A steep gradient of sodium and potassium ions exists at the axon membrane
36. An impulse cannot pass

37. Which of the following indicates the correct path of an electrical impulse through a neuron?
(A) Axon → dendrite → cell body
(B) Dendrite → axon → cell body
(C) Cell body → dendrite → axon
(D) Dendrite → cell body → axon
(E) Axon → cell body → dendrite

Questions 38-40 :

(A) Right ventricle
(B) Aorta
(C) Right atrium
(D) Pulmonary artery
(E) Atrioventricular node

38. The chamber where blood returns to the heart
39. Carries deoxygenated blood to the lungs
40. Causes the walls of the ventricles to contract

Questions 41-44 :

(A) Blood plasma.
(B) Platelets.
(C) White blood cells.
(D) Red blood cells.
(E) Fibrinogen.

41. Responsible for transporting minerals between cells

42. Cells that contain hemoglobin and function in oxygen transport
43. Cells that function in the production of antibodies
44. Cell fragments that function in the blood clotting process
45. Osmoregulation is the maintainance of
(A) Three germ layers.
(B) Body symmetry.
(C) A balance of water and ions
(D) Reproductive fertility
(E) Extra-embryonic membranes

46. All of these cell types contain the diploid (2N) number of chromosomes EXCEPT
(A) Primary oocyte
(B) Spermatogonium
(C) Spermatid
(D) Zygote
(E) Oogonium

47. Progesterone is primarily secreted by the
(A) primary oocyte
(B) hypothalamus
(C) corpus luteum
(D) anterior pituitary gland
(E) endometrial lining

48. Polar bodies are the products of
(A) meiosis in females
(B) meiosis in males
(C) mitosis in females
(D) mitosis in males
(E) two of the above

49. Alchol acts as a diuretic because it
(A) increases secretion of ADH
(B) inhibits the release of ADH
(C) is not reabsorbed by the tubule cells
(D) increases the rate of glomerular filtration
(E) decreases the rate of glomerular filtration

50. A sperm cell only needs to carry genetic information and swim. Which three cell parts are most likely to be found in sperm cells?
(A) Mitochondria, chloroplast, flagellum
(B) Nucleus, ribosomes, mitochondria
(C) Nucleus, chloroplast, flagellum
(D) Nucleus, mitochondria, flagellum
(E) Nucleus, mitochondria, cilia

51. Antidiuretic hormone (ADH) causes which of the following?
(A) Decreased secretions of urea by the kidney
(B) Decreased absorption of glucose by Bowman's capsule
(C) Increased reabsorption of salts by the kidneys
(D) Increased secretions of water by the kidneys
(E) Increased reabsorption of water by the collecting duct

52. Smooth muscle develops from which of the following germ layers?
(A) endoderm
(B) mesoderm
(C) epiderm
(D) ectoderm
(E) none of the above

53. Oogenesis is the process by which
(A) primary oocytes produce sperm
(B) primary oocytes produce eggs
(C) the egg implants in the uterus
(D) the egg is released from the ovary
(E) starfish regenerate limbs

54. A person with blood type (AB) can receive a transfusion from a person with which blood type(s) ?
(A) Type A only
(B) Type A and B
(C) Type B only
(D) Type A, B, and O
(E) Type O only

55. Suppose a vertebrate animal was unable to properly regulate its blood pH. Based on this information, which of the following brain structures is most likely to be damaged?
(A) thalamus
(B) hypothalamus
(C) medulla
(D) cerebellum
(E) cerebrum

56. A lizard in the genus *Cnemidophorus* can reproduce when the female eggs divide mototically without being fertilized by sperm. This type of reproduction is called
(A) Sexual reproduction
(B) Parthenogenesis

(C) Regeneration
(D) Budding
(E) Hermaphrodism

57. Epinephrine and norepinephrine are the fight-or-flight hormones that are released by the
(A) Pituitary gland
(B) Thyroid gland
(C) Adrenal glands
(D) Hypothalamus
(E) Pancreas

58. One of the functions of white blood cells is to ingest and destroy harmful agents, such as bacteria, that find their way into the blood stream. In order to perform this function, you could expect a white blood cell to have a higher than average number of
(A) Ribosomes
(B) Peroxisomes
(C) Chloroplasts
(D) Lysosomes
(E) Chromosomes

59. All of the following are true statements about gametes EXCEPT:
(A) They are haploid cells.
(B) They are produced only in the reproductive structures.
(C) They bring about genetic variation among offspring.
(D) They develop from polar bodies.
(E) They combine to produce cells with the diploid number of chromosomes.

60. Which of the following systems most directly regulate behavioral responses in animals?
(A) Excretory and immune systems
(B) Digestive and endocrine systems
(C) Nervous and skeletal systems
(D) Reproductive and nervous systems
(E) Endocrine and nervous systems

61. Which of the following is LEAST likely to result in a release of adrenaline from the adrenal glands?
(A) walking down a dark, unfamiliar street alone
(B) participating in a highly selective math competition
(C) representing your school at the county track meet
(D) hanging out with your friends after school

(E) being called to your boss's office when you arrive late to work

Questions 62-64 : refer to the graph below, which shows the changes in electric impulse.

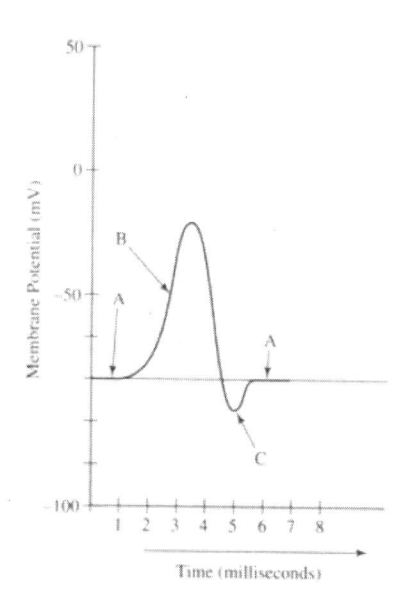

62. Identify where the membrane is **pumping** sodium and potassium ions to in order to return the membrane to the resting potential.
(A) A
(B) B
(C) C
(D) A and B
(E) B and C

63. Identify the action potential
(A) A
(B) B
(C) C
(D) A and B
(E) B and C

64. What is the measurement of the membrane potential at rest?
(A) -100mV

(B) -25mV
(C) -50mV
(D) -70mV
(E) 0mV

65. In non placental mammals, the embryo obtains its food from the
(A) ovary
(B) uterus
(C) oviduct
(D) yolk sac
(E) allantois

66. Which of the following is NOT a direct function of the vertebrate liver?
(A) Synthesis of plasma proteins
(B) Carbohydrate metabolism
(C) Deamination
(D) Reabsorption of water
(E) Detoxification

Questions 67-70 : refer to the following proteins.

(A) Keratin
(B) Hemoglobin
(C) Actin
(D) Insulin
(E) Pepsin

67. This protein requires iron as a cofactor.
68. This protein functions in muscle contraction.
69. This is the principal protein component of skin.
70. This protein functions optimally in high H+ concentrations

Questions 71-72 :

(A) Antibodies
(B) Antigens
(C) T cells
(D) B cells
(E) Histamines

71. Make capillaries more permeable as part of the inflammatory response
72. Are proteins that are found on the surfaces of invading viruses and bacteria

73. Which of these is a correct representation of the hierarchy of biological organization from least to most complex?
(A) organelle of a stomach cell, digestive system, large intestine, small intestine, intestinal tissue, organism
(B) organelle of an intestinal cell, digestive system, small intestine, large intestine, intestinal tissue, organism
(C) molecule, intestinal cell organelle, intestinal cell, intestinal tissue, digestive system, organism
(D) molecule, small intestine, large intestine, intestinal tissue, digestive system, organism
(E) molecule, digestive system, digestive cell organelle, small intestine, large intestine, intestinal cell, organism

74. In human females, the embryo normally implants in the
(A) Ovaries
(B) Fallopian tube
(C) Oviduct
(D) Uterus
(E) Birth canal

75. All of the following are normal functions of the liver EXCEPT
(A) breaks down and recycles red blood cells
(B) removes poisons like alcohol from the blood
(C) produces urea
(D) produces bile
(E) contains bacterial symbionts that produce vitamins

Questions 76-78:

Parathyroid hormone (PTH) is secreted from the parathyroid glands. Under normal conditions, PTH and blood calcium levels are regulated by negative feedback. The normal PTH value is about 100 ng PTH / liter blood, and normal calcium value is about 100 mg calcium / liter of blood. The results of an experiment with PTH are shown below.

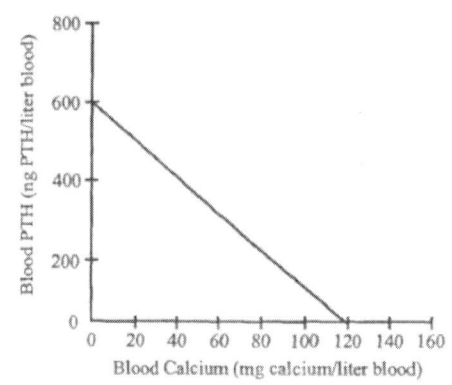

[Graph: Blood PTH (ng PTH/liter blood) vs Blood Calcium (mg calcium/liter blood), showing a decreasing linear relationship from ~600 at 20 mg/L to 0 at ~140 mg/L]

76. Which of the following happen to the PTH level if the parathyroid glands were removed?
(A) Blood PTH would increase.
(B) Blood PTH would decrease.
(C) Blood PTH would fluctuate regularly.
(D) Blood PTH would be secreted by another endocrine gland.
(E) Blood PTH would no longer be needed.

77. Which of the following would happen to the calcium level if the parathyroid glands were removed?
(A) Blood calcium levels would increase.
(B) Blood calcium levels would decrease.
(C) Blood calcium levels would fluctuate regularly.
(D) Calcium would be secreted into the blood by another gland.
(E) Calcium from the blood would be deposited in teeth.

78. What would most likely happen if blood calcium fell to 50 mg calcium / liter blood due to a low-calcium diet?
(A) Blood PTH would decrease.
(B) Blood PTH would not change.
(C) The body would begin processes that would make blood calcium decrease further.
(D) The body would begin processes that would make blood calcium increase
(E) The body could not regulate calcium properly, so there would be no change in the various processes that
regulate blood calcium

Questions 79-82:

(A) Agglutination
(B) Acclimation
(C) Passive immunity
(D) Allergic reaction
(E) Active immunity

79. Protection of a newborn mammal by antibodies from its mother's milk.
80. Symptoms often caused in humans by the release of histamine.
81. The clumping reaction of anti-B antibodies with type B red blood cells.
82. Long-term resistance to chicken pox acquired after infection with chicken pox virus

83. Which of the following would happen to an individual playing a long game of basketball outdoors on a hot afternoon?
(A) The production of thyroxin by the thyroid gland would decrease.
(B) The osmotic pressure of the blood would decrease.
(C) The volume of urine produced would increase.
(D) The concentration of urea in the urine would decrease.
(E) The secretion of antidiuretic hormone from the pituitary gland would increase

84. Which of the following is the correct sequence of events in an action potential after stimulation of a neuron?
(A) K+ moves in; Na+ moves out.
(B) Na+ moves in; K+ moves out.
(C) Na+ moves in; Ca++ moves out.
(D) Na+ moves in; Cl- moves out.
(E) K+ moves in; organic anions move out

85. Which of the following describes an adaptations to arid environment?

(A) A short loop of henle which allows more filtrate to be removed from the blood
(B) A short loop of henle which allows less water to be removed from the filtrate
(C) A long loop of henle which allows more filtrate to be removed from the blood
(D) A long loop of henle which allows more water to be removed from the filtrate
(E) A long loop of henle which allows less filtrate to be removed from the blood

86. The picture above represents some stages in the early development of an embryo. In which of the stages does gastrulation begin?
(A) 1
(B) 2
(C) 3
(D) 4
(E) 5

87. At the neuromuscular junction, which of the following passes from the nerve cell to the muscle cell?
(A) An electrical signal
(B) A chemical signal
(C) A magnetic signal
(D) An axon
(E) A synapse

88. Which of the following is true of the mammalian cardiovascular system?
(A) All arteries contain oxygenated blood
(B) The left side of the heart is completely separated from the right side
(C) The pulmonary and aortic semilunar valves are two-way valves
(D) Blood goes from the right atrium directly to the left atrium
(E) Pulmonary circulation includes the left ventricle and the aorta

89. Which of the following statements about temperature regulation in human living in hot environments is correct?
(A) Perspiration insulates the body and prevents heat loss.
(B) Evaporation of perspiration cools the surface of the skin.
(C) Blood is shunted from the head region to the body cavity.
(D) Blood is more likely to travel near the long bones than near the skin.
(E) Goose bumps cool by decreasing the surface area of the skin.

90. Hemoglobin is a protein in red blood cells that binds and carries oxygen and some carbon dioxide. Its affinity oxygen changes as blood travels from the lungs to the body tissues and back to the lungs again. One could expect hemoglobin to have
(A) A high carbon dioxide affinity in the lungs and a low oxygen affinity in the tissues
(B) A low carbon dioxide affinity in the lungs and a high oxygen affinity in the tissues
(C) A high oxygen affinity in the lungs and a low oxygen affinity in the tissues
(D) A low oxygen affinity in the lungs and a high oxygen affinity in the tissues
(E) A high oxygen affinity in the lungs and a high carbon dioxide affinity in the lungs

91. Excessive acid in the stomach can result in a hole in the wall of the organ. What is this hole called?
(A) Tumor
(B) Cancer
(C) Boil
(D) Ulcer
(E) Hemorrhoid

92. Bile plays an important role in the digestion process because it
(A) Chemically digests starches that would otherwise be eliminated as waste
(B) Controls E. coli activity in the large intestine
(C) Emulsifies fat globules to increase surface area for eventual chemical digestion
(D) Protects gall bladder from infection
(E) Enhances the absorption power of the villi

93. Which of the following is true about the human menstrual cycle?
(A) Fertilization initiates the cycle.
(B) It is regulated by hormones secreted by the adrenal gland.
(C) The endometrium is shed if there is no implantation of an embryo.
(D) It occurs monthly in females throughout their lives.
(E) It is regulated by feedback from the uterus to the ovaries.

(E) Black lung

94. Experiments revealed the following information about molecule Z.
• it is a high molecular weight polymer that can be broken down into amino acids.
• It is capable of breaking down proteins into amino acids.
• it is found in high concentration in the first section of the small intestine.
Which of the following is the most likely source of molecule Z?
(A) Pancreas.
(B) Muscle.
(C) Pituitary.
(D) Testes.
(E) Colon

95. A person with type B blood should not be given a transfusion of type A blood because.
(A) Type AB blood would be formed.
(B) The transfused blood would agglutinate.
(C) Anti-A antibodies destroy anti-B antibodies.
(D) Type A antigens destroy type B antigens.
(E) The type B person would become susceptible to infections.

96. Sensory neurons send impulses down their axons when
(A) They are stimulated by impulses from the spinal cord.
(B) Their cell body releases a neurotransmitter.
(C) They are stimulated by a receptor.
(D) The brain sends signals to them.
(E) The organism is about to do something Dangerous

97. Human lungs contains a protease that helps destroy bacteria that are inhaled and a blocking agent that prevents the protease from digesting the proteins of lung tissue. If the blocking agent is destroyed by tobacco smoke, which of the following diseases would be a direct result?
(A) Pneumonia
(B) Emphysema
(C) Tuberculosis
(D) Influenza

98. Starch-digesting enzymes are secreted into the.
(A) Esophagus only.
(B) Small intestine only.
(C) Small intestine and large intestine.
(D) Mouth and esophagus.
(E) Mouth and small intestine

Questions 99-102: refer to the following terms.

(A) B12 (Vitamin)
(B) Calcium (mineral)
(C) Amylase (enzyme)
(D) Alanine (amino acid)
(E) Testosterone (hormone)

99. An organic nutrient that may serve as a coenzyme in a metabolic reaction.
100. An organic molecule that reduces the energy of activation of a particular metabolic reaction.
101. An inorganic nutrient required for regulatory functions in many cell types.
102. A steroid molecule that regulates one or more metabolic reactions

103. Which of the following components of vertebrate blood is responsible for transporting oxygen?
(A) Red blood cells.
(B) White blood cells.
(C) Serum protein.
(D) Lymph.
(E) Platelets.

104. Lactic acid in humans is a product formed as a result of which of the following processes?
(A) Breakdown of nucleic acids.
(B) Breakdown of protein in digestion activity of muscle cells when oxygen supply is insufficient.
(C) Activity of muscle cells when oxygen supply is insufficient.
(D) Release of stomach acids during development of an ulcer.
(E) Reaction of fats with phosphorus compounds

105. Osmoregulation is the maintenance of
(A) Three germ layers

(B) Body symmetry.
(C) A balance of water and ions.
(D) Reproductive fertility.
(E) Extraembryonic membranes

106. A function of the spleen is to.
(A) Remove damaged cells from blood.
(B) Produce urea.
(C) Manufacture bile.
(D) Destroy cholesterol.
(E) Control the secretion of digestive juices.

107. Fertilization of the human egg normally occurs in the
(A) Uterus.
(B) Fallopian tube.
(C) Ovary.
(D) Vagina.
(E) Vas deferens

108. Which of the following statements is true of most vitamins?
(A) They cannot be synthesized by animals and therefore must be ingested.
(B) They must be present in large amounts to be effective.
(C) They catalyze the digestion of starches.
(D) They have similar molecular structures.

(E) The same vitamins are required by all Animals

109. Which of the following is a function of the cell's plasma membrane?
(A) It inhibits the movement of water into and out of the cell.
(B) It allows diffusion of O_2 but not of CO_2
(C) It traps photons of light
(D) It prevents the diffusion of protein hormones into the cell.
(E) It permits the free movement of starch molecules

Questions 110-111:

The graph below is an oxygen dissociation curve which shows the relative amounts of oxygen bound when the hemoglobin is in solutions with varying partial pressures of dissolved oxygen. The solid line represents adult hemoglobin and the dashed line represents fetal hemoglobin.

110. Based on the graph, when the PO$_2$ is less than 10 mm Hg, which of the following best describes hemoglobin?
(A) It is highly saturated.
(B) It is able to provide a lot more oxygen if metabolism increases.
(C) It transports very little oxygen.
(D) It is at a substantially lower pH.
(E) It is at a somewhat higher pH.

111. Which of the following statements is supported by the data?
(A) The fetal hemoglobin will bind more oxygen at lower oxygen pressure than the mother's hemoglobin.
(B) The mother will be able to unload oxygen for her own tissues before it is available to the fetus.
(C) The fetal tissues require higher oxygen pressure until birth than the maternal constant.
(D) Oxygen pressure in the fetal tissues in nearly constant.
(E) Hemoglobin saturation in the fetal tissues is less variable than in the maternal tissues
(E) Adrenal gland.

113. In the mammalian circulatory system, excess fluid remaining in tissue spaces (interstitial fluid) is:
(A) used to form urine
(B) removed in the form of sweat
(C) drained away by the lymphatic system
(D) moved back into the capillary bed
(E) absorbed by fat cells

Questions 114-115:

(A) Insulin
(B) Growth honnone
(C) Progesterone
(D) Thyroxin
(E) Secretin

114. It directly controls metabolic rate.
115. Its concentration in the blood rises when the corpus luteum develops

116. Hormones released by the posterior pituitary are synthesized by the.
(A) Hypothalamus.
(B) Thalamus.
(C) Anterior pituitary.
(D) Thymus.
(E) Thyroid.

112. During the menstrual cycle of a human female, follicle-stimulating hormone (FSH) and luteinizing hormone (LH) are released from the anterior pituitary. Which of the following is the target organ of both these hormones?
(A) Hypothalamus.
(B) Posterior pituitary.
(C) Uterus.
(D) Ovary.

117. At the neuromuscular junction, which of the following passes from the nerve cell to the muscle cell?
(A) An electrical signal
(B) A chemical signal
(C) A magnetic signal
(D) An axon

(E) A synapse

Questions 118-120 refer to the diagram of the mammalian heart below.

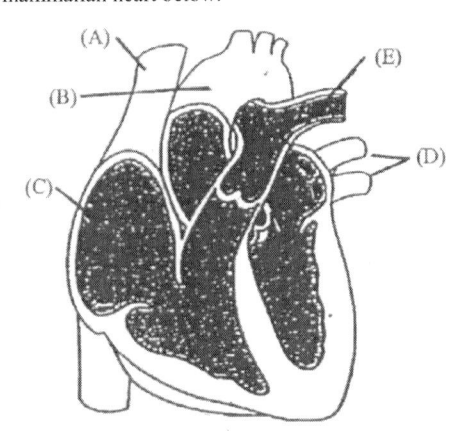

118. Structure that carries deoxygenated blood to the heart.
119. Structure that carries blood to the lungs to be oxygenated.
120. Structure that carries oxygenated blood out of the heart.

121. Which of the following components of vertebrate blood is responsible for transporting oxygen?
(A) Red blood cells.
(B) White blood cells.
(C) Serum protein.
(D) Lymph.
(E) Platelets.

122. Removal of a portion of a person's large intestine would most likely result in.
(A) Watery feces.
(B) Increased vitamin uptake.
(C) Malnutrition.
(D) Indigestion.
(E) Weight gain.

123. Antibodies in humans are produced by which of the following?
(A) Lymphocyte.
(B) Bone marrow.
(C) Red blood cell.
(D) Platelets

(E) Macrophage

124. Nicotine increases the secretion of antidiuretic hormone (ADH) (also known as vasopressin). What is the impact of nicotine on reabsorption of water in the nephron?
(A) Increased reabsorption of water in the descending limb of the loop of Henle.
(B) Decreased reabsorption of water in the descending limb of the loop of Henle.
(C) Increased reabsorption of water in the collecting duct.
(D) Decreased reabsorption of water in the collecting duct.
(E) Increased reabsorption of water in the descending limb of the loop of Henle and in the collecting duct

125. The ......receive(s) blood from the ......and the ....
(A) liver; hepatic arteries; hepatic portal vein
(B) liver; hepatic arteries, hepatic veins
(C) kidneys; renal arteries, renal veins
(D) kidneys; renal arteries; renal portal vein
(E) lungs; pulmonary arteries; pulmonary veins

126. The drug Furosemide is a diuretic. It affects the body's water equilibrium by inhibiting the membrane pumps that actively pump sodium (Na+) and chloride (Cl-) ions across the cell membranes of the ascending limb of the loop of Henle.
What does this drug cause?

(A) Reduced retention of Na+ and Cl- ions in the urine and an *increase* in total blood volume.
(B) Reduced retention of Na+ and Cl- ions in the urine and a *decrease* in total blood volume.
(C) Higher retention of Na+ and Cl- ions in the urine and an *increase* in total blood volume.
(D) Higher retention of Na+ and Cl- ions in the urine and a *decrease* in total blood volume.

(E) No change in the retention of Na+ and Cl- in the urine, but an increase in the total blood volume

127. Why are male animals able to provide gametes with more genetic diversity than females for reproduction?
(A) Males provide more genes in sperm than females provide in eggs.
(B) Male gametes are produced via meiosis, but female gametes are produced via mitosis.
(C) Crossing over occurs more often in the formation of sperm than in eggs.
(D) Spermatogenesis in males results in four functional sperm, while oogenesis in females results in only one egg and three structures that contain genetic information that is lost when they disintegrate
(E) Sperm that contain a recombination of genes are usually more successful in fertilizing an egg.

128. Trypsin and elastase are both enzymes that catalyze the hydrolysis of peptide bonds. Trypsin only cuts next to lysine; elastase only cuts next to alanine. Why?
(A) Trypsin is a protein, and elastase is not.
(B) ΔG for the two reactions is different.
(C) One of the reactions is endergonic, and the other is exergonic.
(D) Hydrolysis of lysine bonds requires water; hydrolysis of alanine bonds does not.
(E) The shape of the active site for the two enzymes is different

129. How does myelination increase the speed that action potentials can travel along an axon?

(A) Myelin insulates the axon from the leakage of ions across the membrane, which allows the action potential to "hop" to the next region of high ion channel density
(B) Myelin conducts the action potentials down the axon by increasing ion channel density.
(C) Myelin decreases intracellular resistance, which causes the action potentials to decay at a *slower* rate.
(D) Myelin decreases intracellular resistance, which causes the action potentials to decay at a *faster* rate.
(E) Myelin increases the membrane resistance and decreases the intracellular resistance, which causes the action potentials to decay at a slower rate

130. A blood vessel has thick muscular walls. This blood vessel is
I. An artery
II. Carrying oxygenated blood
III. Carrying blood away from the heart
(A) I only
(B) III only
(C) I and II only
(D) I and III only
(E) I, II, and III

131. A person becomes anemic when they are not getting enough oxygen to their body. Which of the following could cause someone to be anemic?
(A) A deficiency in white blood cells
(B) A deficiency in red blood cells
(C) A low platelet count
(D) Too little plasma in the bloodstream
(E) An abnormally high T-cell count

132. One of the functions of human white blood cells is to ingest and destroy harmful agents, such as bacteria, that find their way into the bloodstream In order to perform this function, you could expect a white blood cell to have a higher than average number of
(A) Ribosomes
(B) Peroxisomes
(C) Chloroplasts
(D) Lysosomes
(E) Chromosomes

133. Insulin, a protein hormone, must be injected directly into the bloodstream. Why can insulin NOT be taken orally?

(A) It would interfere with the digestion of proteins and fats.
(B) Absorption of insulin by the intestines occurs too slowly, and insulin would degrade by the time it reaches the pancreas.
(C) The acidity of the stomach would denature it, rendering it inactive, after which it would be hydrolysed by pepsin.
(D) It would encounter its hormone antagonist (glucagon) in the digestive tract
(E) In the stomach, the body's immune system would immediately recognize insulin as a synthetic hormone and attempt to destroy it

134. Abnormal functioning what organ is most likely to result in the inability of a person to develop a normal immune response?
(A) Pancreas
(B) Adrenal gland
(C) Thyroid
(D) Pituitary
(E) Thymus

135. Which of the following parts of the vertebrate brain is most closely associated with motor (muscular) coordination?
(A) The hypothalamus
(B) The medulla oblongata
(C) The pineal body
(D) The thalamus
(E) The cerebellum

136. Which of the following statements about temperature regulation in human living in hot environments is correct?
(A) Perspiration insulates the body and prevents heat loss.
(B) Evaporation of perspiration cools the surface of the skin
(C) Blood is shunted from the head region to the body cavity.
(D) Blood is more likely to travel near the long bones than near the skin.
(E) Goose bumps cool by decreasing the surface area of the skin

137. The rate of a human heartbeat is reduced by.
(A) An increase in body temperature
(B) Climbing a flight of stairs
(C) Drinking coffee
(D) Drinking alcohol
(E) Taking amphetamines

138. In humans, proteins are digested by enzymes secreted into the.
(A) Mouth and stomach.
(B) Stomach and small intestine.
(C) Mouth and small intestine.
(D) Stomach and large intestine.
(E) Small intestine only

Questions 139-142 refer to the following proteins.
(A) Keratin
(B) Hemoglobin
(C) Actin
(D) Insulin
(E) Pepsin

139. This protein requires iron as a cofactor
140. This protein functions in muscle contraction
141. This is the principal protein component of skin
142. This protein functions optimally in high H^+ concentrations

143. Which of the following parts of the vertebrate brain is most closely associated with motor (muscular) coordination?
(A) The hypothalamus
(B) The medulla oblongata

(C) The pineal body
(D) The thalamus
(E) The cerebellum

144. Compounds that are foreign to an organism and that elicit an immune response in the organism are called
    (A) antigens
    (B) interferons
    (C) teratogens
    (D) antibodies
    (E) histamines

145. Which of the following hormones is NOT secreted by the anterior pituitary gland?
    (A) Prolactin
    (B) Oxytocin
    (C) Luteinizing hormone
    (D) Thyroid-stimulating hormone
    (E) ACTH hormone

146. Which gland is directly controlled by messages from nerves leading into it?
    (A) Adrenal cortex
    (B) Adrenal medulla
    (C) Anterior pituitary
    (D) Testes
    (E) Ovaries

147. The binding affinity of hemoglobin to O_2 in the bloodstream is greatest at relatively
    (A) High pH and high CO_2 concentration.
    (B) High pH and low CO_2 concentration.
    (C) Low pH and high CO_2 concentration.
    (D) Low pH and low CO_2 concentration.
    (E) Low pH, and does not depend on CO_2 concentration

Questions 148-150 refer to the following mammalian structures.
(A) Oviduct
(B) Uterus
(C) Ovary
(D) Epididymis
(E) Testes

148. Site of implantation of the blastocyst
149. Site of gametogenesis from puberty until death
150. Site of fertilization

151. What is a feature of the human circulatory system?
    (A) The wall of the right ventricle of the heart is the thickest of the four chambers.
    (B) The pulmonary artery and vena cava both carry deoxygenated blood.
    (C) Valves are found in arteries and veins but not capillaries.
    (D) Epinephrine acts on the pacemaker to reduce heart rate
    (E) Aorta carries deoxygenated blood

152. Which describes the secretion of hormones in the pancreas in response to low levels of glucose in the blood?
    (A) Secretion of glucagon from α cells
    (B) Secretion of glucagon from β cells
    (C) Secretion of insulin from α cells
    (D) Secretion of insulin from β cells
    (E) Secretion of FSH

153.

Answers:
1. B
2. B
3. E
4. B
5. A
6. D
7. C
8. E
9. C
10. A
11. E
12. B
13. B
14. E
15. D
16. C
17. D
18. B
19. E
20. B
21. A
22. A
23. C
24. A
25. D
26. B
27. B
28. E
29. B
30. B
31. C

32.D	67.B
33.B	68.C
34.D	69.A
35.A	70.E
36.D	71.E
37.D	72.B
38.C	73.C
39.D	74.D
40.E	75.E
41.A	76.B
42.D	77.A
43.C	78.D
44.B	79.C
45.C	80.D
46.C	81.A
47.E	82.E
48.A	83.E
49.B	84.B
50.D	85.D
51.E	86…….
52.B	87.B
53.B	88.B
54.D	89.B
55.C	90.C
56.B	91.D
57.C	92.C
58.D	93.C
59.D	94.A
60.E	95.B
61.D	96.C
62.C	97.B
63.B	98.E
64.D	99.A
65.D	100.C
66.D	101.B

102.E
103.A
104.C
105.C
106.A
107.B
108.A
109.D
110.C
111.A
112.D
113.C
114.D
115.C
116.A
117.B
118.A
119.E
120.B
121.A
122.A
123.A
124.C
125.A
126………..
127………
128………….
129.A
130.E
131.B
132.D
133.C
134.E
135.E
136.B

137.D
138.B
139.B
140.C
141.A
142.E
143.E
144.A
145.B
146.C
147.C
148.B
149.E
150.A
151.B
152.A

Questions 1-3 :

(A) Phototropism.
(B) Phototaxis.
(C) Gravitropism (geotropism).
(D) Chemotaxis.
(E) Photoperiodism

1. Is shown by bacteria swimming toward a higher concentration of nutrients.
2. Is shown by oat coleoptiles bending toward a source of light
3. Is shown by plant roots growing downward

Questions 4-7 :

(A) Mosses.
(B) Ferns.
(C) Gymnosperms.
(D) Angiosperms.
(E) Fungi

4. Organisms that do not carry out photosynthesis.
5. Organisms that produce flowers.
6. Photosynthetic organisms characterized by absence of conducting tissue.
7. Multicellular organisms responsible for recycling nutrients into the soil

8. Increasing the number of stomata on the upper surface of a leaf would most likely.
(A) Increase evaporation of water from the leaf.
(B) Cause more stomata on the under surface of the leaf to open.
(C) Increase the rate of respiration.
(D) Reduce transpiration.
(E) Prevent the leaves from dropping off in the autumn

9. Which of the following plant cell types is dead at maturity, yet functional?
(A) Parenchyma.
(B) Collenchyma.
(C) Phloem.
(D) Xylem.
(E) Companion cell

10. Sugar synthesized in the leaves of a plant is transported to the roots by way of the
(A) Apical meristem.
(B) Vascular cambium.
(C) Pith.
(D) Xylem.
(E) Phloem

Questions 11-12 :

Refer to the diagram of the fern life cycle shown below for the following questions :

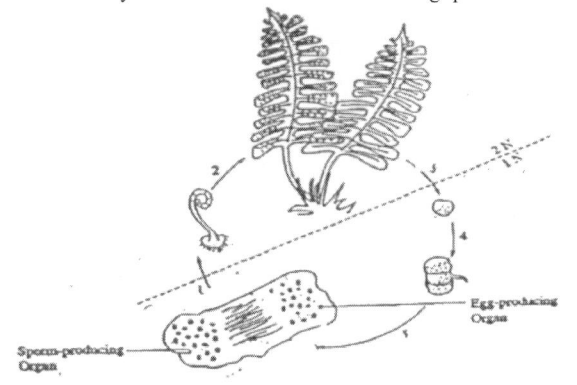

11. Which arrow in the diagram represents the process of fertilization?
    (A) 1
    (B) 2
    (C) 3
    (D) 4
    (E) 5

12. Based on the information in the diagram, which of the following statements is NOT true?

    (A) The found of the new fern plants first emerge rolled up.
    (B) There are two copies of each chromosome in the spore.
    (C) The gametophyte is haploid.
    (D) Gametophytes of ferns are hermaphrodites.
    (E) Ferns form spores

13. The rate of water movement up a tall vascular plant is most dependent on which of the following?
    (A) Root pressure.
    (B) Phloem pressure.
    (C) Transpiration pull.
    (D) Sucrose translocation.
    (E) Rate of photosynthesis

Questions 14- 17 :

(A) Cuticle
(B) Guard cell
(C) Epidermis
(D) Hair
(E) Bristle

14. Controls gas exchange with the environment by responding to short term changes in environmental conditions
15. Lipid layer that reduces water loss at the surface of green plants
16. Reduces wind flow and heat exchange in mammals
17. Cellular layer that separates a vertebrate from its environment

Questions 18-21:

refer to an experiment to test the effects of indoleacetic acid (IAA) on plant growth.
IAA in lanolin was applied to bean cuttings, as indicated in the diagrams below. Apexes were removed in cuttings II through V. All cuttings were suspended in water and allowed to develop roots. The results are shown below. (Lanolin does not affect the biological activity of IAA.)

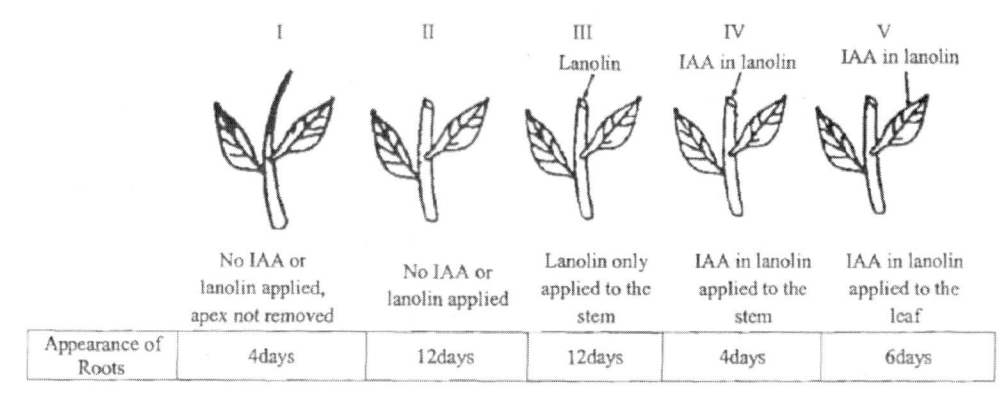

	I	II	III	IV	V
	No IAA or lanolin applied, apex not removed	No IAA or lanolin applied	Lanolin only applied to the stem	IAA in lanolin applied to the stem	IAA in lanolin applied to the leaf
Appearance of Roots	4days	12days	12days	4days	6days

18. Which of the following are the controls for the effect observed with cutting IV?

(A) I and III only.
(B) II and III only.
(C) II and V only.
(D) I, II, and III only.
(E) I, III, and V only.

19. Which of the following most likely accounts for the difference observed between cuttings IV and V?

(A) Not all the apex was removed in cutting V.
(B) Too little lanolin was applied to cutting V.
(C) Diffusion of IAA was slower in cutting IV than in cutting V.
(D) The cuticle and epidermis of the leaf slowed the penetration of IAA into the vascular tissues of the plant.
(E) The enzymes in the leaf destroy the activity of IAA

20. The results obtained from cuttings I, III, and IV suggest that the apex is the normal source of.

(A) Roots cells.
(B) Lanolin.
(C) IAA.
(D) Water.
(E) Nucleic acids.

21. This experiment provides evidence to support the conclusion that IAA stimulates root growth because root growth occurred

(A) At the same time in cuttings II and III
(B) Later in cutting I than in cutting V
(C) Only in cutting IV and V
(D) Earlier in cutting IV than in cutting III
(E) In all cuttings

Questions 22-23 :

Student grew two different flowering plants under the same conditions and found that the piant~ flowered at different times of the year. The student determined that both plants had a critical night length of 13 hours. Plant A only flowered when exposed to a night that was longer than the critical value. Plant B only flowered when exposed to a night that was shorter than the critical value

22. Under the same conditions as before, the student exposed both plants to several days each of a 14-hour dark period and a 10-hour light period. Which of the following would most likely result from this light treatment?

(A) Plant A would flower and plant B would not.
(B) Plant B would flower and plant A would not.
(C) Neither plant would flower.
(D) Both plants would flower
(E) Both plants would die before flowering

23. The student found that a flash of light interrupting the dark period prevents flowering. Under which of the following conditions would plant A still flower?

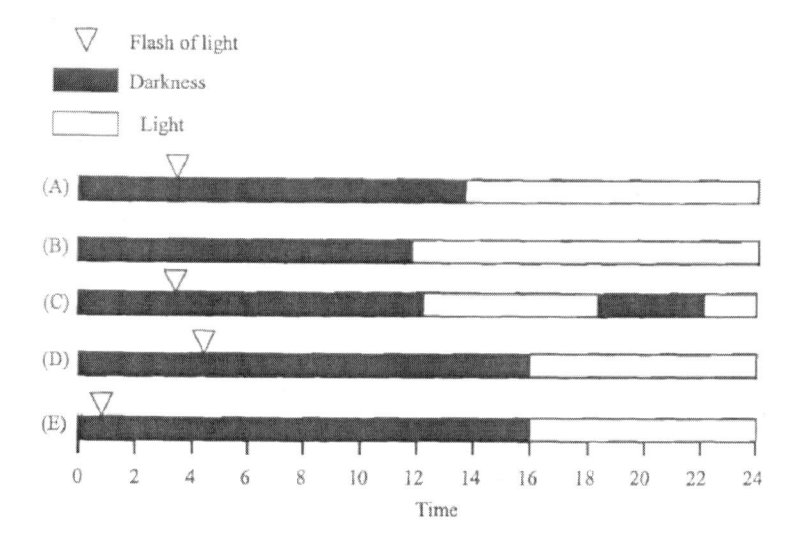

24. All of the following are associated with the Kreb's cycle EXCPT:
(A) Carbon dioxide is produced from the chemical rearrangements of citric acid
(B) Energy is released and used to form ATP molecules
(C) Light energy in the green yellow wavelengths is absorbed and utilized
(D) Specific enzymes for each reaction are found within the mitochondria
(E) Hydrogen ions and electrons are transferred to the carrier NAD⁺

Questions 25-27:

refer to the following diagram A cross section of a corn leaf

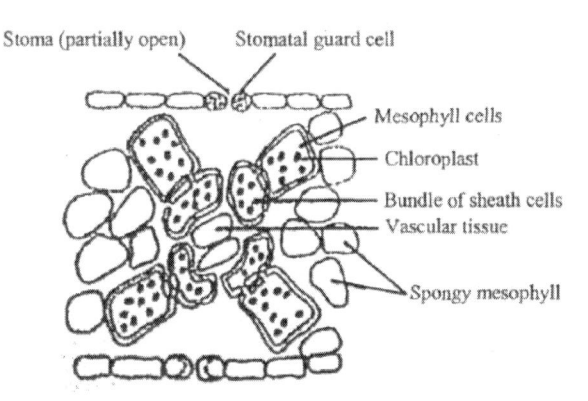

Stoma (partially open)　Stomatal guard cell
Mesophyll cells
Chloroplast
Bundle of sheath cells
Vascular tissue
Spongy mesophyll

25. A difference between the leaf shown and a leaf from the same plant under drought conditions is that under drought conditions, the.
(A) Stomata would be more fully open
(B) Stomata would be mostly closed
(C) Leaf would be greener
(D) Leaf would be more rigid
(E) Mesophyll cells would be swollen

26. The enzymes of the Calvin cycle in this plant are found in which of the following sites?
(A) The cell walls
(B) The mitochondria of mesophyll cells
(C) The vascular tissue
(D) The bundle sheath cells
(E) The epidermis

27. In the diagram, which cells communicate with each other by plasmodesmata?
(A) Stomatal guard cell and epidermal cell.
(B) Vascular tissue and bundle sheath cell.
(C) Mesophyll cell and epidermal cell.
(D) Bundle sheath cell and mesophyll cell.
(E) Spongy cell and epidermal cell

Questions 28- 31:

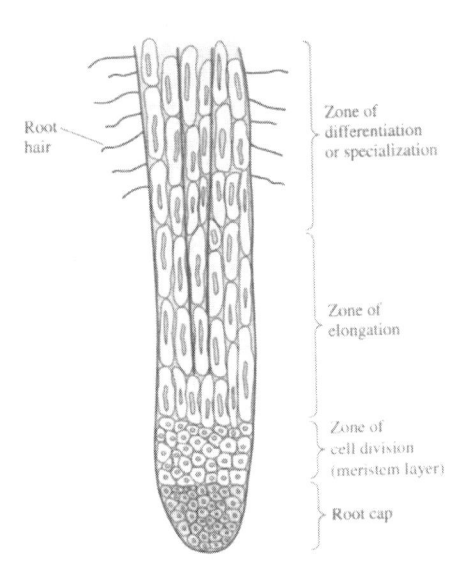

Figure 13.2 Root tip

28. which part is responsible for protection during root growth?
    (A) Root hairs
    (B) Zone of cell division
    (C) Zone of elongation
    (D) Zone of differentiation
    (E) Root cap

29. Which part of the root represents the meristematic cells ?
    (A) Root hairs
    (B) Zone of cell division
    (C) Zone of elongation
    (D) Zone of differentiation
    (E) Root cap

30. The zone at which cells are specialized is
    (A) Root hairs
    (B) Zone of cell division
    (C) Zone if elongation
    (D) Zone of differentiation
    (E) Root cap

31. Help in anchoring and increase surface area for absorption
    (A) Root hairs
    (B) Zone of cell division
    (C) Zone if elongation
    (D) Zone of differentiation
    (E) Root cap

Questions 32-35 :

(A) Gymnosperms
(B) Angiosperms
(C) Algae
(D) Tracheophytes
(E) Nontracheophytes

32. Plants that do NOT make use of xylem and phloem
33. Plants that often need help in order to reproduce
34. Plant group that includes mosses and liverworts
35. Group composed of unicellular protists

36. When a seed is set in the ground, roots will grow downward while stems will grow upward. This plant behavior is an example of
    (A) hydrotropism
    (B) chemotropism
    (C) gravitropism
    (D) thigmotropism
    (E) circadian rhythm

37. Which is vascular tissue associated with phloem?
    (A) vessels
    (B) meristem
    (C) sieve
    (D) tracheids
    (E) sclerenchmya

38. The cells of which of the following structures have a triploid chromosome number?
    (A) pollen
    (B) fruit
    (C) cotyledon
    (D) embryo
    (E) all cells have the diploid chromosome number

39. Which is CORRECT about monocots?
    (A) Vascular bundles in the stem are in a ring.
    (B) Their floral parts are usually in 3s.
    (C) They usually have taproots.
    (D) The veins in the leaves are netlike.
    (E) Most common trees, such as maples and oaks, are monocots.

40. Conifers and flowering plants are classified in the same phylum. Which of the following characteristics do they share?
(A) They are all perennials.
(B) The xylem is dead at maturity.
(C) They are all woody plants.
(D) They both contain seeds.
(E) They both shed their leaves.

41. Which of the following structures is NOT part of the pistil?
   (A) Ovule
   (B) Ovary
   (C) Style
   (D) Anther
   (E) Stigma

42. The plant tissue that gives girth to a plant during each growing season is called the
(A) phloem
(B) tracheid
(C) secondary xylem
(D) lateral meristem
(E) apical meris tem

43. All of the following are examples of tracheophytes EXCEPT
(A) trees
(B) moss
(C) grass
(D) corn
(E) beans

Questions 44-47 :

(A) Phototropism
(B) Photoperiodism
(C) Thigmotropism
(D) Gravitropism

44. . Plant growth toward a light source
45. When a Venus flytrap snaps shut in response to an insect
46. Growth of a plant in response to the direction of gravity
47. Biological effects caused by changes in day length

47.
Structural components common to plant cell walls but not part of bacterial cell walls include which of the following?
   I. Peptidoglycan
   II. Cellulose
   III. Lignin
(A) I only
(B) II only
(C) I and III only
(D) II and III only
(E) I, II, and III

48. Elongation of cells in shoot tips of plants is promoted by
   (A) abscisic acid
   (B) carotene
   (C) cytokinin
   (D) ethylene
   (E) auxin

49. The euglena possesses an organelle that synthesizes a polysaccharide for storage. This organelle is the
   (A) stigma
   (B) pyrenoid
   (C) eyespot
   (D) cytopharynx
   (E) oral groove

50. Leguminous plants such as soy beans and peas exhibit a mutualistic symbiosis with
   (A) Herbivores
   (B) Bacteria
   (C) Other leguminous plants
   (D) Humans
   (E) Soils

51. Which of the following is an actively dividing tissue in plants?
   (A) Cambium
   (B) Xylem
   (C) Endodermis
   (D) Phloem
   (E) Pith

52. Root hairs are extensions of which of the following kinds of cells?
   (A) Cortical
   (B) Xylem
   (C) Phloem
   (D) Epidermal
   (E) Meristematic

53. In which of the following stages does a fern contain vascular tissue?
(A) Spore
(B) Sporophyte
(C) Gamete
(D) Gametophyte
(E) Archegonium

54. Cellular respiration shares which of the following characteristics with the light-dependent reactions of photosynthesis?
(A) Production of A TP
(B) Production of AMP
(C) Production of GTP
(D) Production of oxygen
(E) Use of carbon dioxide in synthetic reactions

Questions 55-57 refer in the following figures.

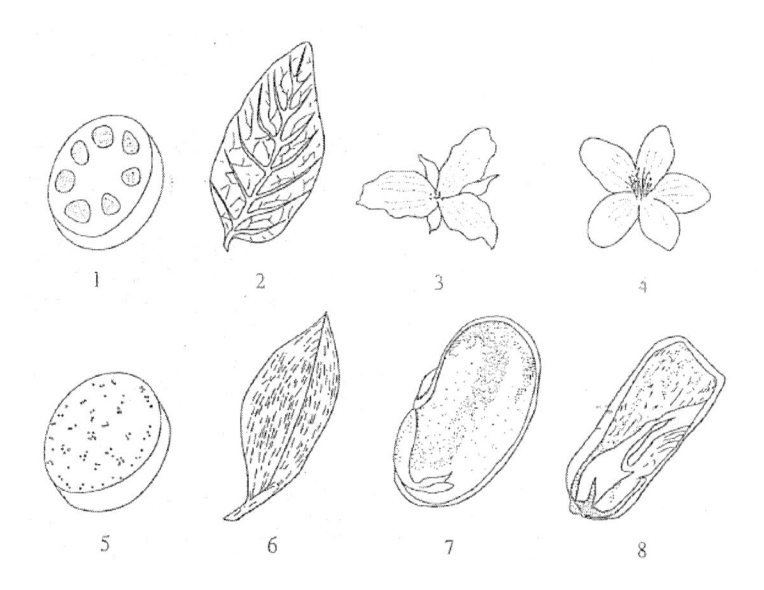

55. Numbered structures that contain pistils and stamens include which of the following?
(A) 3 only.
(B) 7 only.
(C) 2 and 3 only.
(D) 3 and 4 only.
(E) 7 and 8 only.

56. Which of the four numbered structures represent dicots?
(A) 1 ,2,4, and 7
(B) 1 ,2,5, and 6
(C) 2,3,4, and 6
(D) 2,5,6, and 7
(E) 3,5,6, and 8

57. Which of the following paired structures are the major organs of photosynthesis?
(A) 1 and 4.
(B) 2 and 6.
(C) 3 and 4.
(D) 3 and 5.

(E) 7 and 8.

Questions 58-59

Refer to the diagram of the fern life cycle shown below for the following questions.

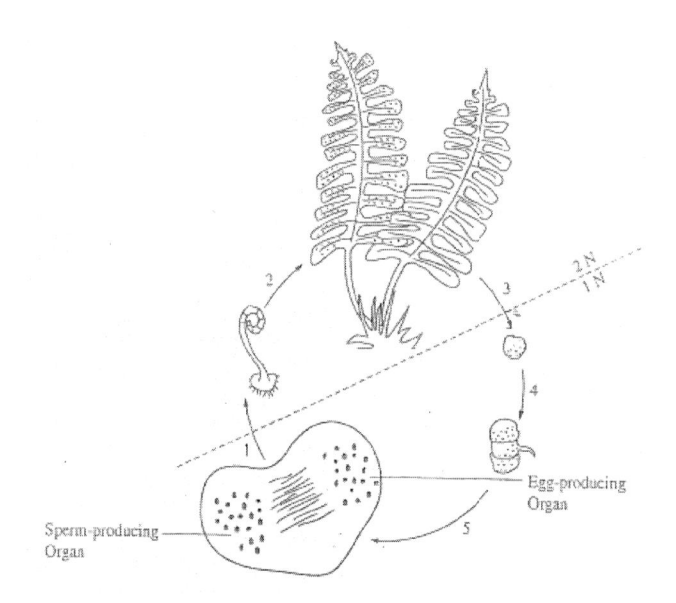

58. Which arrow in the diagram represents the process of fertilization?
(A) 1
(B) 2
(C) 3
(D) 4
(E) 5

59. Based on the information in the diagram, which of the following statements is **NOT** true?
(A) The found of the new fern plants first emerge rolled up.
(B) There are two copies of each chromosome in the spore.
(C) The gametophyte is haploid.
(D) Gametophytes of ferns are hermaphrodites
(E) Ferns form spores

Questions 60-64:

Observations of the respiration rate of pea seedlings at different temperatures over time produced the following data. The rates are given as a percentage of the rate at 25°C

Temperature	0 hr	1 hr	2 hr	3 hr	4 hr	5 hr	6 hr	7 hr	8 hr
0 °C	100%	60%	40%	10%	10%	10%	10%	10%	10%
10° C	100%	75%	60%	40%	40%	40%	40%	40%	40%
25 °C	100%	100%	100%	100%	100%	100%	100%	100%	100%
30 °C	100%	110%	130%	140%	140%	140%	140%	140%	140%
40 °C	100%	130%	140%	170%	160%	150%	140%	130%	120%
50 °C	100%	98%	96%	94%	70%	45%	30%	15%	0%

60. If the rate at 30°C is plotted against time, a graph of the results would look like which of the following?

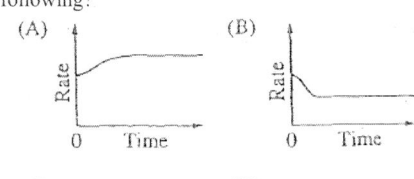

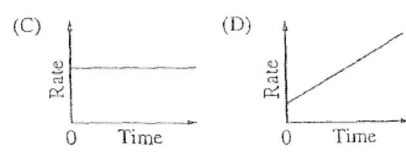

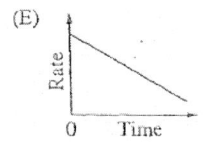

(A)
(B)
(C)
(D)
(E)

61. If a reading were taken at 7.5 hours at 40°C, the rate most likely would be
(A) 110%
(B) 120%
(C) 125%
(D) 130%
(E) 135%

62. The control-temperature in the experiment is
(A) 0 °C
(B) 10 °C
(C) 25°C
(D) 30°C
(E) 50 °C

63. According to the data, a pea seedling is most likely to die in 8 hours at which of the following temperatures?
(A) 0 °C
(B) 10°C
(C) 25°C

(D) 40°C
(E) 50°C

64. Based on the data, the best explanation for the respiration rate after 3 hours at 0°C is that
(A) enzymes hydrolyze at low temperatures
(B) low temperatures slow down reaction rates
(C) enzymes are not affected by temperature changes
(D) enzymes are used up within 3 hours
(E) enzymes are inactivated by the changes in pH that occur at 0 °C

65. All of the following functions are performed by roots EXCEPT:
(A) Storage.
(B) Mineral absorption.
(C) Cell reproduction.
(D) Anchorage.
(E) Leaf production.

66. Which of the following occurs in many angiosperms, but NOT in many vertebrates?
(A) Sexual reproduction
(B) Carbohydrate storage
(C) Cellular respiration
(D) Protein synthesis
(E) Asexual reproduction

67. Fertilizers that are applied to soils contain which of the following substances essential for the growth and development of plants?
(A) Vitamins.
(B) Inorganic compounds.
(C) Carbohydrates.
(D) Proteins.
(E) Lipids

68. Which of the following adaptive features would be found in flowering plants that live in an arid climate?

(A) Vascular tissues

(B) Stomates

(C) Thick cuticles

(D) Multiple leaves

(E) Megaspores

69. Which of the following best accounts for the ability of legumes to grow well in nitrogen-poor soils?

(A) These plants make their own proteins

(B) These plants have a mutualistic relationship with nitrogen-fixing bacteria

(C) These plants are capable of directly converting nitrogen gas into nitrates

(D) These plants do not require nitrogen to make plant proteins

(E) These plants have developed nitrogen-absorbing root hairs

70. All of the following adaptations that directly enable terrestrial plants to maintain water balance EXCEPT
(A) Waxy cuticle
(B) Xylem
(C) Stomata
(D) Root hairs
(E) Chloroplasts

72. Mycorrhizal fungi are available for purchase by farmers and home gardeners. These fungi are predicted to have a major impact on how we grow our food in the coming decades. How do these fungi benefit growers?
(A) They interact with plant roots to provide water and nutrients to the plant
(B) They act as an inexpensive and effective fertilizer, providing the plant with nutrients as fungi decompose
(C) The fungi attract pollinators, counteracting declining bee populations
(D) They produce mushrooms, which reduce the need for irrigation by reducing evaporation
(E) They discourage aphids and other insects from feeding on the plants

73. What is the effect of abscisic acid on transpiration?
(A) Decreases transpiration by causing stomata to close.
(B) Increases transpiration by causing stomata to open.
(C) Decreases transpiration by causing roots to absorb less water.
(D) Increases transpiration by causing roots to absorb more water.
(E) Abscisic acid has no effect on transpiration rates.

74. Transpiration occurs in 200-meter tall redwood trees primarily because:

(A) Root pressure pushes the water up
(B) Evaporation of water through the stomata pulls water up
(C) Gravity creates pressure within xylem
(D) Photosynthesis in the leaves requires water
(E) Water naturally moves from roots to Leaves

75. The diagram below shows a cross-section of a plant stem. What is the labelled structure and one of its functions?

	Structure	Function
a.	Xylem	Gas exchange
b.	Phloem	Transport of sugars
c.	Pith parenchyma	Gas exchange
d.	Xylem	Transport of water
e.	Phloem	Gas exchange

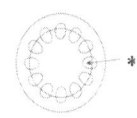

Questions 76-80:

(A) Binary fission
(B) Budding
(C) Spore formation
(D) Vegetative propagation
(E) Parthenogenesis

76. Reproduction of bacteria
77. Possible production of seedless fruit
78. Reproduction of yeast cells
79. Development of an egg without a sperm
80. An example is an underground stem with buds

81. Plants are broadly defined as multicellular, photosynthetic eukaryotes. Which of the following is NOT an additional feature of this group?
(A) Plants can respond to changes in day length.

(B) Plants have cell walls containing cellulose.
(C) Plant chloroplasts contain chlorophyll A and chlorophyll B.
(D) Plants have starch as the primary storage carbohydrate.
(E) Plant respiration is mostly anaerobic.

82. Which of the following structures offers the same advantages to plants that the shell of an egg offers to reptiles and birds?
(A) Flower.
(B) Xylem.
(C) Cork cambium.
(D) Seed coat.
(E) Spore capsule

Questions 83-85: refer to the following phenomena
(A) Phototropism.
(B) Phototaxis.
(C) Gravitropism (geotropism).
(D) Chemotaxis.
(E) Photoperiodism.

83. Is shown by bacteria swimming toward a higher concentration of nutrients.
84. Is shown by oat coleoptiles bending toward a source of light
85. Is shown by plant roots growing downward

Questions 86-89:

(A) Mosses.
(B) Ferns.
(C) Gymnosperms.
(D) Angiosperms.
(E) Fungi.

86. Organisms that do not carry out photosynthesis.
87. Organisms that produce flowers.
88. Photosynthetic organisms characterized by absence of conducting tissue.
89. Multicellular organisms responsible for recycling nutrients into the soil.

90. Which of the following plant cell types is dead at maturity, yet functional?
(A) Parenchyma.
(B) Collenchyma.
(C) Phloem.
(D) Xylem.
(E) Companion cell

91. Sugar synthesized in the leaves of a plant is transported to the roots by way of the
(A) Apical meristem.
(B) Vascular cambium.
(C) Pith.
(D) Xylem.
(E) Phloem.

92. The rate of water movement up a tall vascular plant is most dependent on which of the following?
(A) Root pressure.
(B) Phloem pressure.
(C) Transpiration pull.
(D) Sucrose translocation.
(E) Rate of photosynthesis. .

93. Communication across plant cell walls occurs by mean of the
(A) Nucleus
(B) Ribosomes
(C) Endoplasmic reticulum
(D) Plasmodesmata
(E) Gap junction

94. Leguminous plants, such as soybeans and peas, exhibit a mutualistic symbiosis with certain
(A) Carnivores.
(B) Bacteria.
(C) Other leguminous plants.
(D) Humans.
(E) Soils

95. the number of stomata on the upper surface of a leaf would most likely.
(A) increase evaporation of water from the leaf.
(B) Cause more stomata on the under surface of the leaf to open.
(C) Increase the rate of respiration.
(D) Reduce transpiration.
(E) Prevent the leaves from dropping off in the autumn

Questions 96-99:

(A) Xylem.
(B) Phloem.
(C) Stomata.
(D) Epidermis.
(E) Mesophyll

96. Tissue in which most photosynthesis takes place.
97. Tissue in which organic nutrients are transported.
98. Tissue in which water minerals are transported.
99. Tissue with a cuticle layer.

100. Woody plants with tall, straight main stems that have few branches may be made to develop bushier forms by.
(A) Applying fertilizer heavily and frequently
(B) Shading the plants to reduce the amount of light received.
(C) Watering the plants frequently.
(D) Severely pruning the root systems.
(E) Removing the terminal buds

101. plants that form flowers that are not brightly colored and that lack fragrance are most likely pollinated by.
(A) Bees.
(B) Wind.
(C) Birds.
(D) Butterflies.
(E) Flies.

102. A tree stands 6 meters high and is 0.20 meter in diameter. A branch falls leaving a scar that is 0.90 meter above the ground. In 20 years if the tree is 36 meters high, that scar will be how far from the ground?
(A) 18.00 meters
(B) 12.00 meters
(C) 7.20 meters
(D) 6.00 meters
(E) 0.90 meter

103. The main advantage in planting a legume such as soybeans in a field one year and corn in the same field next year is that legume

(A) Use less water than com does
(B) Produce more oxygen than com does
(C) Increase the aeration of the soil
(D) Increase the nitrogen content of the soil
(E) Increase the phosphorus content of the soil

104. Which of the following colors of light is LEAST likely to be absorbed by an ordinary plant leaf?
(A) Violet
(B) Blue
(C) Green
(D) Yellow
(E) Red

105. The trunk of a dicot tree grows in diameter largely from cell divisions that occur in Ihe
(A) Apical meristem
(B) Vascular cambium
(C) Cortex
(D) Phloem
(E) Xylem

106. The diagram represents the life cycle of a fern, with the stages drawn to different scales.

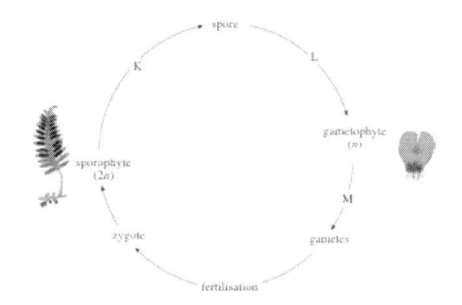

Which one of the rows A to E correctly represents the nuclear events occurring at stages K, L and M?

	K	L	M
A.	mitosis	meiosis	mitosis
B.	mitosis	mitosis	meiosis
C.	mitosis	meiosis	meiosis
D.	meiosis	meiosis	mitosis
E.	meiosis	mitosis	mitosis

Answer Key (Plants):

1. D
2. A
3. C
4. E
5. D
6. A
7. E
8. A
9. D
10. E

11. A
12. B
13. C
14. B
15. A
16. D
17. C
18. D
19. D
20. C
21. D
22. A
23. E
24. C
25. B
26. D
27. D
28. E
29. B
30. D
31. A
32. E
33. B
34. E
35. C
36. C
37. C
38. C (The cotyledon (3n) results from the fusion of one sperm nucleus (n) and two polar bodies (2n). A seed consists of an embryo (2n), which resulted from fertilization of the ovum (n) and a sperm nucleus (n))
39. B (Monocots have floral parts oriented in 3s and have parallel veins in the leaves. Dicots usually have taproots, and the veins in their leaves are netlike. Most trees are dicots. Palm trees are monocots)
40. D
41. D
42. D
43. B
44. B
45. D
46. E
47. C
48. D (**Cellulose** and **lignin** are structural components unique to plant cells. These materials serve supportive functions. Peptidoglycan, also called murein, is a complex structure consisting of polysaccharide chains connected by short sequences of amino acids. This substance composes part of the bacterial cell wall, but it is not present in plant cells)
49. E
50. C
51. B
52. A
53. D
54. D
55. D
56. A
57. B
58. A
59. C
60. A
61. C
62. C
63. E
64. B
65. E
66. E
67. B
68. C
69. B
70. E

Protein synthesis

1. Different stages of protein synthesis are given below.
    - (A) A – Movement of mRNA from nucleus to cytoplasm
    - (B) B – Linking of adjacent amino acid molecules.
    - (C) C – Transcription of mRNA from a DNA template
    - (D) D – Formation of polypeptide chain
    - (E) E – Attachment of mRNA strand to a ribosome

    Which of the following is the correct sequence of events in protein synthesis?
    - (A) A, C, B, E, D
    - (B) A, E, C, D, B
    - (C) C, A, E, B, D
    - (D) C, D, A, B, E
    - (E) E, A, D, C, B

Questions 2-5:
- (A) Replication
- (B) Recombination
- (C) Transcription
- (D) Translation
- (E) Deletion

2. A DNA strand serves as a template for the synthesis of another DNA strand of equal length.
3. DNA serves as a template for the synthesis of a new molecule of RNA.
4. Two DNA molecules exchange corresponding segments.
5. An RNA molecule provides directions for the assembly of protein.

6. The human genome is estimated to contain 30,000 expressed genes. This means that there are approximately 30,000
    - (A) Chromosomes in each human cell
    - (B) DNA molecules in each human cell
    - (C) Different proteins possible in a human
    - (D) Copies of one gene
    - (E) Nucleotide base pairs in human DNA

7. A function of transfer RNA is to
    - (A) receive the genetic information from nuclear DNA
    - (B) store the genetic information in the nucleus
    - (C) store RNA in the ribosomes
    - (D) transfer the genetic information from the nucleus to the cytoplasm
    - (E) position amino acids for protein synthesis by pairing with codons in mRNA

8. The nitrogenous base, adenine, is found in which three of the following
    - (A) Proteins, chlorophyll, and vitamin A
    - (B) Protein, ATP, and DNA
    - (C) ATP, DNA, and RNA
    - (D) Chlorophyll, ATP, and DNA
    - (E) Proteins, carbohydrates, and ATP

Answers:

1.C

2.A

3.C

4.B

5.D

6.C

7.E

8.C

Taxonomy

1. Which of the following is an important difference between algae and fungi?
(A) Algae photosynthesize; fungi do not.
(B) Algae have true roots; fungi do not.
(C) Algae reproduce by a sexual means only; fungi reproduce both sexually and asexually.
(D) Algae are always green; fungi occur in several colors.
(E) Algae are heterotrophic; fungi are autotrophic.

2. Which of the following has more energy per photon than visible light, and can be seen by some insects but not by humans?
(A) Infrared radiation.
(B) Solar radiation.
(C) Gamma radiation.
(D) Ultraviolet radiation.
(E) Ionizing radiation.

3. Which statement about taxonomic relationships is **CORRECT**?
   (A) A class can contain more than one phylum
   (B) A genus can contain more than one order
   (C) A family can contain more than one class
   (D) An order can contain more than one family
   (E) A genus can contain more than one family

4. Which of the following is a characteristic of an open circulatory system?
i. Heart
ii. Arteries
iii. Capillaries
iv. Veins
   (A) i only
   (B) i, ii, and iv
   (C) i and iii
   (D) i, ii, iii, and iv
   (E) ii and iv

5. Which of the following is used by female moths to attract males?
(A) Warning coloration.
(B) Vocalization.
(C) Shape.
(D) Body temperature.
(E) Pheromones.

Questions 6-9:
(A) Monera
(B) Protista
(C) Fungi
(D) Plantae
(E) Animalia

6. Contains all the protozoa and most of the algae
7. Contains multicellular heterotrophic organisms that reproduce asexually by spores
8. Contains organisms without membrane-bound organelles such as nuclei
9. Contains autotrophic organisms with cells that are organized into tissues and organs

Questions 10-12

(A) Cnidarians
(B) Chordates
(C) Annelids
(D) Round worms
(E) Flat worms

10. Radial symmetry
11. Two cell layers thick
12. Three cell layers thick but have no coelom

Questions 13-17: are based on the following phylogenetic tree. Pick the letter on the branch that matches the most likely placement of the taxon

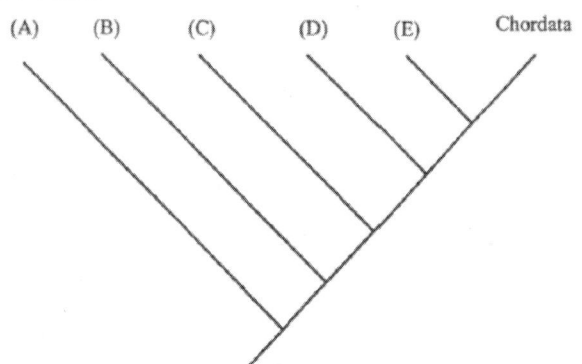

(A) (B) (C) (D) (E)   Chordata

13. Echinodermata E
14. Archaea A
15. Protista C
16. Planta D
17. Fungi B

18. All of the following are characteristics of the members of the phylum Chordata **EXCEPT**.
(A) Bilateral symmetry
(B) A dorsal, hollow nerve chord
(C) An external skeleton
(D) Gill slits in some developmental stage
(E) A notochord at some developmental stage

19. Rapid motility is normally associated with animals that
(A) Have radial symmetry.
(B) Have bilateral symmetry.
(C) Have biradial symmetry.
(D) Are asymmetrical.
(E) Are spherical

20. Which of the following occurs in many angiosperms, but NOT in many vertebrates?
(A) Sexual reproduction.
(B) Carbohydrate storage.
(C) Cellular respiration.
(D) Protein synthesis.
(E) Asexual reproduction.

21. Which of the following organisms is adapted to thrive in salt marshes (high salt environment)?
(A) Eubacteria
(B) Fungi
(C) Archae bacteria
(D) Protozoa
(E) Algae

22. Which of the following is true of archaebacteria (Archaea)?
(A) They are made up of eukaryotic cells.
(B) They generally inhabit the most hospitable environments on Earth.
(C) They share chromosomal characteristics with Eukarya.
(D) They are multicellular.
(E) They are much more dominant than they were 3 billion years ago

23. Adaptations found in reptiles that enable them to be completely terrestrial include which of the following?
I. A leathery amniotic egg
II. Extensive parental care
III. Water tight skin
(A) I only.
(B) II only.
(C) III only.
(D) I and III only.
(E) I, II. and III

24. Recent taxonomic trees have shown that giant pandas should be classified with bears (family Ursidae), but that lesser pandas are more closely related to raccoons (family Procyonidae). Data from which of the following types of studies would provide the best evidence of relationships for the panda species?
(A) Comparison of feeding behaviors and use of limbs.
(B) Comparison of blood proteins and DNA-DNA hybridizations.
(C) Comparison of the litter sizes of the animals.
(D) Comparison of present-day native habitats.
(E) Comparison of fur coloration.

25. The classification of organisms into different kingdoms is based on which of the following?
(A) The structure of the organisms' cells and, how the organisms obtain nutrition
(B) The typical habitats of the organisms.
(C) Whether the organisms are motile.
(D) How the organisms reproduce.
(E) How long the organisms have been

26. Which of the following vertebrates belongs to the class Amphibia?
(A) Snapping turtle.
(B) Shark.
(C) Swordfish.
(D) Salamander.
(E) Crocodile

27. Which of the following cellular structures can be used for locomotion?
I. Cilia.
II. Flagella.
III. Microvilli.

(A) I only
(B) II only
(C) III only
(D) I and II only ✓
(E) I, II, and III

28. All Arthropods contain:
   (A) cuticle, abdomen without legs, bilateral symmetry
   (B) double nerve cord, gonads and ducts, haemocoel
   (C) triploblastic body, malpighian tubules, mouth parts
   (D) complete alimentary canal, dorsal ganglia, trachea
   (E) larval stages, unisexual animals, cilia

29. Why is maintaining a high body temperature (e.g., 37°C) more challenging for smaller endothermic animals than for larger endothermic animals?
   (A) Smaller animals have a lower metabolic rate (per gram of body mass) relative to larger animals.
   (B) Smaller animals have a *higher* surface area to volume ratio and therefore lose greater amounts of heat to the environment ✓
   (C) Smaller animals have *lower* surface area to volume ratio and therefore lose greater amounts of heat to the environment
   (D) Smaller animals are unable to produce enough brown adipose tissue whereas larger animals can
   (E) Smaller animals are unable to shiver at a rate that is fast enough to produce heat in their muscles

30. Which statement about this phylogenetic tree is CORRECT?
   (A) Humans are equally closely related to cats and frogs
   (B) Lizards and cats are more closely related than lizards and humans
   (C) Fish are the most recent common ancestor of the other organisms in the tree
   (D) Geese and fish are more closely related than geese and frogs
   (E) Frogs are equally closely related to cats and lizards

31. I am unicellular. I am autotrophic. I swim with a flagellum. I possess a nucleus. My cell wall lacks both chitin and peptidoglycan. Who am I?
(A) A fungus
(B) A bacterium
(C) A protist ✓
(D) An archaeon
(E) A flowering plant

Questions 32-35:

A copperhead **snake**: (Agkistrodon contortrix) and a **canary** (Serinus canarius) are both being studied in a zoological laboratory

32. During the night, the air temperature in the lab falls. What happens to the two organisms' metabolic rates?
(A) Both remain stable
(B) Both increase
(C) snake's decrceases canary's remains stable ✓

(D) Both decrease
(E) Canary's decreases, snake's increases

33. The copperhead has tiny leg bones along its skeleton. These structures are
(A) Mutations
(B) Homologous
(C) Analogous
(D) Vestigial
(E) Convergent

34. All of the following are true about endotherms **EXCEPT**
(A) They inhabit a wide range of environments
(B) They typically become more active with warmer temperatures
(C) They maintain body temperatures higher than their surroundings
(D) They are all heterotrophs
(E) They evolved relatively later than ectotherms

35. Which of the following distinguishes the canary from the copperhead?
(A) Four-chambered heart
(B) Thick-shelled eggs for survival on land
(C) Vertebral column
(D) Bony skeleton
(E) Closed circulatory system

36. If biological success is measured by species diversity, distribution, and number of individuals, which of the following groups would be considered the most successful?

(A) Mammals
(B) Arthropds
(C) Echinoderma
(D) Fish
(E) Mollusks

37. Mechanisms used by mammals to lower body temperature include all of the following **EXCEPT**
(A) Burrowing
(B) Changing posture
(C) Panting
(D) Flapping ears
(E) Exercising vigorously

38. Kangaroos are classified as mammals because they have which of the following characteristics?
(A) Live young
(B) Placental incompletion
(C) Prescence of special glands for production of milk
(D) Prescence of external pouch for development of the young
(E) Well-developed parental care

39. Which of the following has more energy per photon than visible light, and can be seen by some insects but not by humans?
(A) Infrared radiation.
(B) Solar radiation.
(C) Gamma radiation.
(D) Ultraviolet radiation.
(E) Ionizing radiation.

40. Which of the following is an important difference between algae and fungi?
(A) Algae photosynthesize; fungi do not.
(B) Algae have true roots; fungi do not.
(C) Algae reproduce by a sexual means only; fungi reproduce both sexually and asexually.
(D) Algae are always green; fungi occur in several colors.
(E) Algae are heterotrophic; fungi are autotrophic.

41. Which of the following is a vertebrate that **does NOT** have a bony skeleton?
(A) Frog
(B) Shark
(C) Monkey
(D) Snake
(E) Hawk

Questions 42-44 refer to the following diagram of a circulatory system.

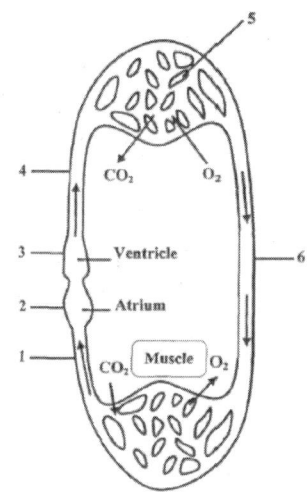

42. The circulatory system diagrammed could be that of which of the following animals?
(A) Fish
(B) Bird
(C) Snake
(D) Salamander
(E) Frog

43. The structure that is most closely analogous to the lung of a dog is
(A) 1
(B) 2
(C) 3
(D) 5
(E) 6

44. In which of the following is the concentration of carbon dioxide **lowest**?
(A) 1
(B) 2
(C) 3
(D) 4
(E) 6

45. Which of the following adaptations in vertebrates enabled them to colonize early terrestrial environments successfully?
(A) Lungs, efficient kidneys, amniotic eggs
(B) Ovaries and testes, wings, four-chambered heart
(C) Backbone, teeth, waterproof skin
(D) Binocular vision, closed circulatory system, lungs
(E) Efficient kidneys, four-chambered heart, Scales

46. In vertebrates, the bony endoskeleton performs which of the following functions?

I. It protects internal organs.
II. It serves as a site for muscle attachment.
III. It serves as a reservoir for calcium.
(A) I only
(B) II only
(C) I and II only
(D) II and III only
(E) I, II, and III

47. . One important adaptation that developed in terrestrial arthropods such as insects, but not in aquatic arthropods; such as crayfish, and that allowed the insects to invade the terrestrial environment is
(A) Jointed appendages
(B) Digestive system
(C) Tracheal respiratory system
(D) Muscular system
(E) Central nervous system

48. An earthworm and a snake both possess which of the following characteristics?
(A) Radial symmetry
(B) Dorsal tubular nervous system
(C) Closed circulatory system
(D) Chitinous exoskeleton
(E) Scales

49. True statements about the development of the frog and mouse embryos include which of the following?

I. Both the frog and the mouse embryos develop in an aqueous environment.
II. Both the frog and the mouse embryos depend on a large supply of yolk to sustain the developing embryo.
III. Both the frog and the mouse embryos develop a 4-chambered heart.

(A) I only
(B) III only
(C) I and II only
(D) II and III only
(E) I, II, and III

50. The photograph shows an animal of the species *Eisenia fetida*.

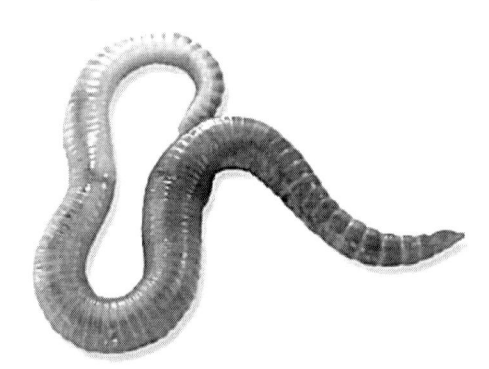

Which phylum does it belong to?

(A) Cnidaria
(B) Platyhelminthes
(C) Annelida
(D) Arthropoda
(E) Chordata

Answers:
1. A
2. D
3. D
4. B
5. E
6. B
7. C
8. A
9. D
10. A
11. A
12. E
13. E
14. A
15. C
16.….D
17.……B
18. C
19. B
20. E
21. C
22. C
23. D
24. B
25. A
26. D
27. D
28. C
29. B
30.……
31. C
32. C
33. D
34. C
35. A
36. B
37. E
38. C
39. D
40. A
41. B
42. A
43. D
44. E
45. A
46. E
47. C
48. C
49. C
50. C

college Board
855-373-6387

Manufactured by Amazon.ca
Acheson, AB